MURDER IN
MONTAGUE

MURDER IN
MONTAGUE

———————

FRONTIER JUSTICE
AND RETRIBUTION IN TEXAS

GLEN SAMPLE ELY

UNIVERSITY OF OKLAHOMA : NORMAN

Publication of this book is made possible through the generosity of Edith Kinney Gaylord.

Library of Congress Cataloging-in-Publication Data

Names: Ely, Glen Sample, author.
Title: Murder in Montague : frontier justice and retribution in Texas / Glen Sample Ely.
Description: Norman : University of Oklahoma Press, 2020. | Includes bibliographical references
and index. | Summary: "The wholesale slaughter of the England family in August 1876 near
Montague, Texas, and subsequent courtroom trials present a vivid and searing snapshot of
frontier justice and retribution in Texas following the Civil War, as the state transitioned
from vigilantes and lynching toward an established criminal justice system"—Provided
by publisher.
Identifiers: LCCN 2020003823 | ISBN 978-0-8061-6709-1 (paperback)
Subjects: LCSH: Murder—Texas—Montague—History—19th century. | Trials (Murder)—
Texas—Montague—History—19th century. | Criminal justice, Administration of—Texas—
History—19th century.
Classification: LCC HV6534.M775 E47 2020 | DDC 364.152/309764541—dc23
LC record available at https://lccn.loc.gov/2020003823

To Helen Scanlon Sample
and John Glen Sample

CONTENTS

ACKNOWLEDGMENTS

Without the help of a number of people, this book would not have been possible. I thank Margaret and Roscoe Conkling for an obscure reference in their 1930s research files (now housed at the Seaver Center, Museum of Natural History, Los Angeles) that originally led me to this case. Donaly Brice, former historian at the Texas State Library and Archives, located a number of vital documents for me. Marci Ellen Spivey provided the Texas Court of Appeals cases. Halley Grogan, photo archivist at the Texas State Library and Archives, kindly supplied photos, as did Michelle Lambing of the Texas State Preservation Board. Sandra Rogers, archivist at the Texas Prison Museum in Huntsville, Texas, generously gave a great deal of her time to provide me with advice, period prison accounts, records, and photos. Texas legal historian Michael Ariens, professor at St. Mary's University School of Law, graciously spent much time reviewing the manuscript and providing detailed advice, perspective, and analysis on the state's nineteenth-century criminal justice system. Texas author Bill Neal and retired FBI Special Agent Phil Walters also read the manuscript, offering excellent suggestions for improvement. Cartographer Tom Jonas produced the England-Krebs land map.

My thanks also go to the district clerks of Cooke County and Montague County, Texas; the county clerk of Montague County, Texas; Barbara Whiteley and the County Clerk's Office in Scott County, Arkansas; the Coal County (Oklahoma), Genealogical Society; John Terrill and the Scott County (Arkansas) Historical and Genealogical Society; Joy Russell and the Madison County (Arkansas) Genealogical and Historical Society; Patrick and Carolyn Timlin; Larry Richardson; David Rumsey Historical Map Collection (for use of the 1886 map of Texas); Patricia Ann Newman, who supplied much assistance, genealogy advice, and Krebs family pictures; William Preston "Little Bill" Krebs, who offered family pictures and granted me several interviews; Cheryl Rivera, who provided her mother's, Joyce Whatley's, family genealogy book; L. Hodges, who lent me her picture of Luna Music; and Trent Shotwell, special collections librarian, Newton Gresham Library, Sam Houston State University, Huntsville, Texas, who supplied Huntsville photos. I am also very grateful to Ralph Wilson Veatch for taking me to Vinita, and to Gregory Charles Nelsen, Bryan Keith Touchstone, Daniel L. Penner, J. Keith Miller, Elizabeth "Lisa" Taylor Ely, Diane Drayton Rzegocki, Delfina Isabel Ely, Francisca Ely Bali de Zamora, Col. Anthony R. Ely, Timothy Strong Ely, Alfred L. Bush, Charles B. Johnson II, Mark Andrew Traver, Col. Thomas "Ty" Smith, Robert Wooster, Jerry D. Thompson, David Owen Sanders, Kim Allen Nuzzo, Daniel Ray Luenberger, Ron and Nancy Sorensen, Lorne and Emily Prescott, and Melinda Ann Veatch for all of their kindness and support. Lastly, many thanks to J. Kent Calder, acquisitions editor, Kirsteen Anderson, copyeditor, and Stephanie Attia Evans, assistant managing editor, at the University of Oklahoma Press, for all their fine work on behalf of this book.

CAST OF CHARACTERS

William Hampton Taylor–Wiley Savage–Ben Krebs Families

William Hampton Taylor: Born in 1818 in Missouri, William married Jane Barnett, who was born in 1823 in South Carolina. William and Jane's children were William Barnett "Bill" Taylor, Aaron Kendrick Taylor, and Eliza Ann "Rhoda" Taylor.

William Barnett "Bill" Taylor: Born in 1853 in Missouri, he was the son of William Hampton Taylor and Jane Barnett Taylor. His siblings were Aaron Kendrick Taylor and Eliza Ann "Rhoda" Taylor.

Aaron Kendrick Taylor: Born in 1860 in Texas, Aaron was the son of William Hampton Taylor and Jane Barnett Taylor. He was brother to William Barnett "Bill" Taylor and Eliza Ann "Rhoda" Taylor.

Eliza Ann "Rhoda" Taylor Savage Krebs: Born in 1843 in Missouri, Rhoda was the daughter of William Hampton Taylor and Jane Barnett Taylor and sister of William Barnett "Bill" Taylor and Aaron Kendrick Taylor. Her first marriage, in 1857, was to Wiley Blount Savage, who died in 1864. Rhoda and Wiley had several children, including Mary Jane Savage and John Wiley Savage. Her second marriage, in 1865, was to Ben Krebs. Rhoda's and Ben's children included Georgia Ann "Annie" Krebs and William Benjamin Krebs.

Wiley Blount Savage: Born in 1812 in Tennessee, Wiley first married Mary A. Carney, who died in 1850. His second marriage was to Eliza Ann "Rhoda" Taylor in 1857. His children were Thomas N. Savage, Mary Jane Savage, and John Wiley "Johnnie" Savage. He died in 1864.

Thomas N. Savage: Born in 1838 in Tennessee, Thomas was the son of Wiley Blount Savage and Mary A. Carney.

John Wiley "Johnnie" Savage: Born in 1864 in Montague County, Texas, Johnnie was the son of Wiley Blount Savage and Eliza Ann "Rhoda" Taylor Savage. He was living with Ben and Rhoda Krebs in 1876.

Mary Jane Savage: Born in 1860 in Montague County, Texas, Mary was the daughter of Wiley Blount Savage and Eliza Ann "Rhoda" Taylor Savage. She was living with Ben and Rhoda Krebs in 1876.

Ben Krebs: Born in 1828 in Switzerland, Ben emigrated to the United States in 1850 and lived in Wisconsin. By 1857, Krebs had moved to Belknap, county seat of Young County, Texas. In 1865 Krebs married Eliza Ann "Rhoda" Taylor Savage. Ben's and Rhoda's children included Georgia Ann "Annie" Krebs and William Benjamin Krebs.

Georgia Ann "Annie" Krebs: Born in 1870 in Montague County, Texas, Annie was the daughter of Ben and Rhoda Krebs.

William Benjamin Krebs: Born in 1866 in Montague County, Texas, William was the son of Ben and Rhoda Krebs and the father of William Preston "Little Bill" Krebs.

James Preston Family

James Preston: Born in 1823 in Tennessee, James married Martha Elizabeth Rice in Missouri in 1847. During their marriage James and Martha had ten children. They were friends and former neighbors of Ben and Rhoda Krebs.

Martha Elizabeth Rice Preston: Born in 1828 in Tennessee, Martha was the wife of James Preston. She died in February 1876, in Montague County, Texas.

Billington Taylor–William England Families

Billington Taylor: *No relation to the William Hampton Taylor family.* Born in 1820 in Tennessee, he married Selena (maiden name unknown) in 1836. By 1855, they had moved to Texas. Children from their marriage included Sue

Anne "Susie" Taylor, Isaiah Taylor, and Harvey Taylor. Billington Taylor died in 1866 or 1867.

Selena Taylor England: Selena was born in 1820 or 1821 in Kentucky; her maiden name is unknown. In 1836, she married Billington Taylor in Jefferson County, Illinois. By 1855, the Taylors had moved to Texas. Children from their marriage included Sue Anne "Susie" Taylor, Isaiah Taylor, and Harvey Taylor. Following Billington's death, Selena married her neighbor William England in 1870. In 1875, the couple, along with Selena's children, moved from Grayson County to Montague County, where they were neighbors of Ben and Rhoda Krebs and John and Luna Music.

Isaiah Taylor: Born in 1843 in Illinois, Isaiah was the son of Selena and Billington Taylor and stepson of William England.

Harvey Taylor: Born in 1849 in Illinois, Harvey was the son of Selena and Billington Taylor and stepson of William England.

Sue Anne "Susie" Taylor: Born in 1855 in Texas, Susie was the daughter of Selena and Billington Taylor and the stepdaughter of William England.

William England: Born in 1794 in Virginia, William worked as a Methodist minister and farmer. His first marriage was to Chloe Pike in 1817 in Tennessee. William and Chloe had eight children. Chloe died in 1870. In 1870, William was living in Whitesboro, Grayson County, Texas. In December 1870 he married his neighbor Selena Taylor.

John Music Family

John R. Music: Born in Arkansas in 1849, John was the son of William Granville Music and Louisa Perkins Music. During his childhood John lived in Montague County, Texas. In the 1860s, he relocated to Hunt County, Texas. There, he met Luna Broderick Smith, whom he married in 1869. In 1876 John, with his wife and children, moved back to Montague County, where they were neighbors of the Krebs and England families.

Luna Broderick Smith Music Dickerson: Born in 1849 in Illinois, Luna was the daughter of William Daniel Bohning Smith and Rebecca Minerva Bird Smith. By 1860, the Smith family had moved to Hunt County, Texas, where Luna met John R. Music. Married in 1869, Luna and John had three children during the 1870s: Minerva Elizabeth, Louisa Belle, and William Daniel, who died at age two. Luna later married Bonam Franklin Dickerson.

Lawyers and Lawmen

Avery Lenoir Matlock: Born in 1852 in Blount County, Tennessee, Avery moved to Montague, Texas, in September 1873. Elected Montague County attorney in 1875, he served from 1875 to 1878. He was elected to the Texas House of Representatives in 1880 and to the Texas State Senate in 1882. The 1882–83 *Texas Legislative Manual* noted, "As county attorney, Mr. Matlock has received the credit of having convicted some of the worst criminals that have infested the state." In 1887, the owners of the XIT Ranch in Texas hired him as a legal investigator. During the 1880s and 1890s, Matlock served as complainant's attorney in numerous Indian depredation cases filed in the U.S. Court of Claims. He subsequently started a law practice in San Antonio in 1906, where he later served as city attorney. Matlock died in 1933 and is buried at Oakwood Cemetery in Fort Worth.

Lee N. Perkins: Lee was the sheriff of Montague County, Texas, in 1876.

Joseph Alexander Carroll: Joseph was born in Missouri in 1832 and was elected judge of Texas's Sixteenth Judicial District in 1876. The Sixteenth District encompassed Denton, Tarrant, Parker, Jack, Wise, Montague, Clay, and Cooke counties.

William H. Grigsby: A partner in the Grigsby & Willis Law Firm, William was co-counsel for Ben Krebs, James Preston, and Aaron K. Taylor. Grigsby was admitted to the bar in 1862 at Lexington, Missouri, and had formerly served as the Montague County attorney. He was the brother of James M. Grigsby, who served as the county judge of Ochiltree County, Texas, from 1921 to 1930.

Frank Willis: Frank received his law license in Liberty, Kansas, in 1869. He was later district attorney in Independence, Kansas. In 1875 Willis relocated to Montague, Texas, and started a law practice with William H. Grigsby. Frank and William were co-counsels for Ben Krebs, James Preston, and Aaron K. Taylor. In 1881, Governor O. M. Roberts appointed Frank as district judge of the Thirty-First Judicial District in the Texas Panhandle.

— 1 —

Saturday August 26, 1876, was a typical sweltering summer day in North Texas. That night, a half-moon illuminated the sky. Methodist minister William England and his wife, Selena, had spent the evening at their beautiful new home six miles south of Montague, Texas, with Isaiah, Harvey, and Susie Taylor, three of Selena's children from her first marriage. William, eighty-two years of age, was from Virginia. Selena, fifty-six, was a Kentucky native. The Englands had recently moved to Montague County from Whitesboro in Grayson County. The family had occupied much of their time after dinner on Saturday discussing the pending nuptials of thirty-three-year-old Isaiah. The hour was late when they decided to turn in. Before heading to bed, Reverend England and his family said their prayers.[1]

The August night was stifling, so twenty-seven-year-old Harvey Taylor decided to sleep on a pallet on the front porch in hopes of catching a cool breeze. The rest of the family went indoors and got ready to retire. While reclining on his makeshift bed, Harvey saw three men walking down the Montague-Decatur Road toward the England homestead. At first glance, he thought they were his brothers Joseph, Isaac, and Birch, who lived nearby. The smallest of the three approached the house and opened the front gate, which was ten feet from the porch. The other two remained behind the gate and were "crouching down as if to conceal themselves."[2]

The uninvited visitor stepped up onto the porch where Harvey was resting on his mattress. The man, now clearly visible in the moonlight, came within two or three feet of Taylor. He brandished a pistol in Harvey's face and barked at him, "Goddamn you, get in the house." Harvey quickly complied, rising from his pallet and entering the England home. Once inside, Harvey walked into the north bedroom, where he spotted his brother Isaiah standing in the doorway between the north and south bedrooms.[3]

The armed intruder, following right behind Harvey, saw Isaiah and growled at him, "Goddamn you, I told you that I would kill you and now I intend to do it." The man pointed his pistol at Isaiah and shot him. As Isaiah fell to the floor, Harvey bolted for the back door. On his way out, Harvey "heard another shot in the house, and then . . . several [more] shots, and men cursing and women screaming. After the screaming he heard more shots, and then heard no more noise of any kind." Harvey kept running, passing through a field, until he reached the home of the Williards, neighbors who lived a quarter mile away.[4]

Back at the England residence, a grisly slaughter was underway. Selena England later told the local doctor, J. E. Stinson, that when the gunman shot Isaiah in the hallway of their home, she and her twenty-one-year-old daughter Susie Taylor rushed out of the house. The assailant followed close behind, pistol in hand. Both women believed that the man pursuing them was "old Ben Krebs," a neighbor who lived a half mile distant. The pair climbed over the yard fence and raced for the corral gate, with the gunman following, "shouting at us, and cursing us all the time." The terrified mother and daughter were screaming constantly now, and Susie cried out, "Mother, old Ben Krebs is come to kill us all." Selena recalled that Krebs replied, "God damn you, you need not scream; I have come to kill you and God damn you, I am going to do it."[5]

Their attacker managed to get between them and the corral gate, effectively blocking their escape. With Susie holding onto her mother, the pair turned and ran back toward the front porch gate on the west side of the house. The gunman followed, firing his pistol and cursing at them. One shot struck Selena. She hit the fence and fell to the ground. "I did not see Susie anymore," she said, "but in a moment I heard Susie cry out, 'Oh, mother, Krebs has killed me.'" After a few minutes lying in the yard, Selena had recovered somewhat when she heard her husband, William, calling out her name.[6]

Selena told Dr. Stinson that although she was severely wounded, she managed to get up and head toward the house, with Krebs in pursuit once again. Upon entering the home, she saw her husband sitting in a chair by the wall. One of the

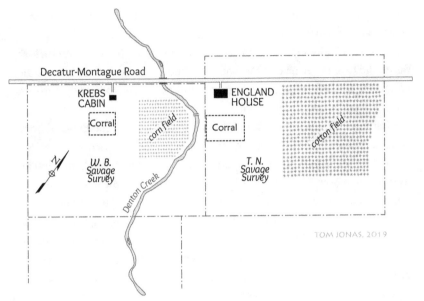

Decatur-Montague Road

KREBS CABIN

ENGLAND HOUSE

Corral

corn field

Corral

cotton field

N

W. B. Savage Survey

T. N. Savage Survey

Denton Creek

TOM JONAS, 2019

Detail of the Krebs and England properties, six miles south of Montague, Texas. *Map by Tom Jonas.*

other intruders stood behind him, "pulling his head back by the hair and cutting his throat with a knife." After taking in this macabre spectacle, Selena fled out of the house with her assailant still following her, out the back door and into the garden, whereupon she fainted from her wounds.[7]

When she awoke, she was alone. Selena managed to get up and limp the half mile across a cotton field toward the home of other neighbors, John and Luna Music. She reported passing out several times along the way, but eventually reached the Musics, who took her into their house and immediately sent for Dr. Stinson. Stinson received the summons shortly before midnight. When he examined Selena a short time later, he found that "she was shot in the back, and the ball [bullet] had passed out at her breast. She was mortally wounded, and perfectly conscious that she would die."[8]

Dr. Stinson conversed at length with Selena England and "found her perfectly rational." During their conversation, Selena told Stinson, "Old Ben Krebs has killed me and my family." She said "that when Krebs shot her, she was close enough to him to have put her hands in his whiskers." Selena also stated that the man who killed her husband was either Krebs's friend James Preston or a "Dutchman" who had stopped at her home the previous day.[9]

After rousing Dr. Stinson, John Music went to E. T. Vanhooser's house for additional help. Upon arriving at the Music residence, Vanhooser found Selena England "very badly shot," but "in her right mind" and fully cognizant that "she was bound to die." Selena told Vanhooser, "I know that old Ben Krebs has killed me and my whole family." She exhorted Vanhooser "to go to Krebs's house and arrest him and all the others there."[10]

After hearing Selena's account, Vanhooser journeyed to the England home, where he encountered a chilling tableau of death. Vanhooser discovered Reverend England's body lying in a pool of blood. He had been shot through the chest and his throat had been slit with a knife. "There was blood on the floor of the north room and two streams of blood" leading to where the body lay. On both sides of the north room door "were the prints of bloody fingers, scraping down each side of the door, as if the old man had tried to hold himself up while sinking down." Vanhooser found Susie Taylor, who had been gunned down, lying dead on the walk between the porch and the gate. A few hours later, at sunrise on the morning of Sunday, August 27, Vanhooser spotted Isaiah Taylor's corpse sprawled out in the Montague-Decatur Road, forty yards south of the England home. He had also been shot.[11]

Meanwhile, at the Williard home, Selena's son Harvey Taylor was describing the attack to Mr. and Mrs. Williard. At two in the morning, Harvey and the Williards went to the England home. The Williards stopped at the front gate while Harvey went inside the pitch-black house alone. He lit a candle and saw much of what Vanhooser had witnessed: his stepfather lying facedown on the floor with blood everywhere, and the lifeless body of his sister Susie on the walkway in front of the porch. Because it was still dark during his visit, Harvey was unable to find his brother Isaiah.[12]

At nine in the morning on Sunday, August 27, twenty-four-year-old Montague County Attorney Avery Lenoir Matlock and several others journeyed to the England home to make a detailed investigation of the crime scene. Matlock interviewed the mortally wounded Selena, who had been carried from the Music home to a back bedroom in the England residence early Sunday morning. Matlock bent over Selena and whispered in her ear, asking her if she knew who had slaughtered her family. Selena England was completely rational, knew who Matlock was, and understood that she would soon die. She repeated what she had previously told Dr. Stinson and E. T. Vanhooser; namely, that one of the men who had attacked her family was Ben Krebs and another was either James Preston or a Dutchman who had stopped at her home the day before the murders.[13]

Outside the house, a large crowd of curious onlookers had gathered. Among the throng were Selena's immediate neighbor to the south, forty-eight-year-old Ben Krebs, and Krebs's friend and former neighbor, James Preston, who had spent the previous evening at Krebs's home. The fifty-three-year-old Preston was a Tennessee native who in 1872 had purchased land bordering both the Krebs and England properties.[14]

After questioning Selena, Matlock immediately went outside and arrested Krebs and Preston. Then he and Montague County Sheriff Lee N. Perkins tracked down the Dutchman in question and brought him to the England home. Matlock and Perkins took the man before Selena, who said he was not the second killer, whereupon he was released. It was later confirmed that the itinerant immigrant was simply passing through the area on his way to a nearby settlement and was not involved in the murders.[15]

Next, the county attorney had Sheriff Perkins bring Krebs inside Selena's bedroom for identification. Matlock asked Selena if Krebs was the person who had shot her. When she answered "yes," Krebs replied, "You must be mistaken; it must be your imagination." He repeated this statement three or four times. Selena admonished Krebs, "Don't you feel mighty bad about killing my poor children and my poor husband?" Krebs again replied that she was making a mistake, that she was imagining things.[16]

Selena countered, "I am not mistaken; I was close enough to you to put my hand in your whiskers, if I had wanted to. I knew you by your whiskers," she said, "I knew your face; I knew your Dutch talk; I knew your curses; and I even recognized that old white hat you now hold in your hand." Krebs repeatedly denied her charges and wanted to talk more, but before he could do so, he was removed from Selena's bedroom and taken back outside. Inexplicably, Matlock and Perkins neglected to take James Preston before Selena for identification.[17]

Sheriff Perkins then transported Krebs and Preston to Montague, where he locked them in the county jail. Selena England died a day later, on the morning of Monday, August 28. Relatives took the bodies of Reverend England, Selena, Susie Taylor, and Isaiah Taylor back to Grayson County, their previous county of residence, and buried them in Ben Dye Cemetery near Whitesboro. Each of the four graves featured a bright red sandstone slab. Newspapers across the state adopted a melodramatic and macabre tone in their coverage of the case. On August 29, the *Denison Daily News* reported, "Wholesale slaughter near Montague. Murdered in cold blood . . . by masked men. . . . A murder most foul. . . . A fiendish outrage. The opinion prevails that they [the Englands] were murdered for money, as the family was known to be well off, having just completed a fine house."[18]

The *Austin Weekly Democratic Statesman* reported that a Montague County family who lived near Denton Creek had been viciously murdered. The killers, "Cribbs [*sic*] and party," had "dyed their hands in the blood of a neighbor; a minister of the gospel," and his son. "Not yet satisfied with this cruel act," they refused to spare the weak and innocent, slaying the mother and daughter, "victims of a murderous midnight cruelty."[19]

The *Galveston Daily News* headline blared, "The fiendish murder of a whole family in Montague County. . . . Mrs. England has since died but stated before her death that Ben Cribs [*sic*], a neighbor, was one of the murderers. He has been arrested, but bitterly denies the charge. The excitement is high, and it is thought Cribs will be lynched."[20]

Authorities soon arrested a third individual, sixteen-year-old Aaron Kendrick Taylor, the brother of Rhoda Taylor Krebs, Ben's wife. Aaron and Rhoda were from a different Taylor family, unrelated to Selena and her children. On the night of the murders, Aaron was visiting the Krebs home and slept over there. Selena England never mentioned Aaron Taylor nor implicated him in the killings; nevertheless, County Attorney Matlock locked him up in the Montague jail with Krebs and Preston. Selena and her son Harvey both stated that three men had been involved in the murders. Because Aaron Taylor had been with Preston at Krebs's home that night, county officials reasoned he must have been that third person.[21]

In their survey of the murder scene, Matlock and five others scoured the area around the England home for clues. At the north end of the England residence they found one set of tracks from a size 8 or size 9 shoe, with a worn-down heel on the left shoe. In between the house porch and the gate, they located the same set of tracks following behind the tracks of two barefooted persons with small feet. Selena England and Susie Taylor had both been barefoot on Saturday night. Next, Matlock and his assistants discovered three sets of shoe imprints nearby in the Englands' cotton field.[22]

Expanding their search area, the men came upon footprints from the same size 8 or 9 shoe with a worn-down heel crossing the Montague-Decatur Road and in Ben Krebs's cornfield, coming to within 150 yards of Krebs's home. At this spot, two other sets of shoes joined the worn-down heel. The second shoe was also a size 8 or 9, and the third, a size 5 or 6. For the next one hundred yards, all three sets of shoes traveled a parallel course to a point fifty yards from the Krebs residence. It was here that the trackers lost all three trails in the tall grass and weeds. The search party concluded that these three sets of shoe impressions exactly matched those found earlier in the Englands' cotton field.[23]

Matlock and his associates measured all three sets of tracks with a ruler but neglected to take casts or molds of the imprints. After finishing at the England home, the county attorney returned to the Montague jail and measured the shoes of the three prisoners with the same ruler. In his opinion, their shoes exactly fit the three sets of tracks he had measured near the England and Krebs homes. Ben Krebs wore a size 8 or 9 with a worn left heel. Preston also wore size 8 or 9 brogans, while Taylor's were size 5 or 6 with boot-like heels. Matlock's learned opinion, however, obscured sloppy police work. He had been in such a rush to arrest and jail the suspects that he had neglected to check the suspects' shoes while they were still at the England home to see if they matched the shoeprints found on the ground. Therefore, his judgment that the shoes he measured in jail were an exact fit with the shoeprints at the crime scene could not be positively proven and was ultimately an inference.[24]

After examining the prisoners' shoes in the county jail, Matlock turned next to the question of motive. What possible reason could Krebs, Preston, and Taylor have had for committing such a gruesome slaughter? Krebs appeared to have had a motive for killing the England family. In July 1876, a month before the murders, he had almost come to blows with Reverend England over England's hogs getting into Krebs's cornfield. Krebs had menacingly threatened England with a fencepost several times during the incident. William and Selena England subsequently filed an aggravated assault charge against Krebs that was pending in court, a charge that could cost Krebs dearly and possibly send him to jail. Since three men committed the murders, and Preston and Taylor had spent the night at Krebs's house, Matlock reasoned that they must have been Krebs's accomplices. Matlock now had his case ready to present to the grand jury.[25]

The *Galveston Daily News* complimented the young county attorney for his handling of the case. Matlock, "as soon as he heard of the murder, repaired to the scene and was not long in taking in the whole situation, had the guilty parties arrested and used his official and personal influence to prevent violence." The *News* also commended local citizens for allowing justice to take its course rather than resorting to vigilantism. The paper remarked, "The good people of Montague County deserve credit for not lynching the murderers of the England family. For black-hearted fiendishness that certainly outstripped any crime which has been committed in this country, and the proof was positive, yet the people preferred to permit the law to assert her supremacy."[26]

$$= 2 =$$

The sheer brutality of the England family murders terrified frontier settlers already traumatized by decades of chaos, violence, and fear. From the 1850s to the 1870s, area residents contended with Indian depredations, vigilante mobs, sectional tensions, murders, lynchings, and rampant lawlessness. For some, the nighttime slaughter of the England family rekindled vivid, painful memories of numerous Indian raids on local ranches and farms. During this period Comanches and Kiowas assaulted North Texas counties near the Red River at will and without warning. Young, Jack, Wise, Montague, and Cooke Counties all had their share of grisly, brutal attacks.

Notable Indian incidents were the Elm Creek Raid and Warren Wagon Train Massacre in Young County; the Mason-Cambern Massacre, Thurman Spring Raid, and Lost Valley Fight in Jack County; the Babb, Russell, and Huff Massacres in Wise County; the Keenan-Paschal Massacre and Denton Creek Fight in Montague County; and the Box and Clear Creek Massacres in Cooke County. Many citizens had personally witnessed the gruesome carnage inflicted in these strikes. Some had lost kinfolk and close friends. Several representative examples provide a clearer understanding of what families living on the North Texas frontier confronted.[1]

It was just after bedtime on a winter night in 1870 when nine Indians forced their way into a log cabin near Uz, in southeastern Montague County. Inside were two German families, the Keenans and Paschals. The raiders shot Mrs. Keenan in her bed, scalped her, then cut her throat "from ear to ear." Next, they clubbed Mrs. Paschal to death, lanced her, and mutilated her body. Nine-year-old Will Paschal was beaten to death, stabbed repeatedly, and his right arm cut off. Six-year-old John Paschal was lanced and disemboweled. The Indians also killed John Keenan and his eight-year-old daughter.[2]

Three years later, in September 1873, Mortimer Stevens, Howell Walker, and his son Henry Walker were busy hauling water at Thurman Spring, seven miles southwest of Jacksboro, in neighboring Jack County. Within minutes, Indian warriors surrounded the three men at the waterhole. Stevens managed to escape, but Howell and Henry Walker were not so fortunate. The raiders shot the father's chest full of bullets, took his entire scalp, and gutted his body from back to front, leaving his bowels and entrails hanging out. The Indians also took a rib from his right side. Son Henry was found scalped, lying on his back with the stump of his arm sticking up. His hand had been cut off. Reading numerous period accounts such as these, one senses that the net cumulative effect of a quarter century of violent atrocities and the constant anxiety of not knowing when and where the next raid might occur, must have scarred the psyches of area residents with some degree of posttraumatic stress disorder.[3]

From the onset, Indian depredations and endemic regional violence had distressed settlers moving to the North Texas frontier. Prior to the Civil War, regional federal outposts at Fort Belknap and Camp Cooper helped mitigate the frequency of these attacks while preserving the expanding line of European American settlement. When Texas seceded in February 1861, the U.S. Army withdrew its troops from the Lone Star State. During the Civil War, the situation significantly worsened. Confederate and Texas state troops proved unable to adequately defend the state's frontier due to a lack of men and resources. Chronic attacks by Comanches, Kiowas, and white renegades caused the western edge of settlement to recede by 100 to 150 miles.[4]

North Texas's frontier line began collapsing in early 1863 when Texas Ranger Captain James Diamond in Gainesville reported Indians and outlaws were raiding the region and residents were on the verge of fleeing eastward. Diamond warned that without immediately increased protection, area settlements would dissolve "and the whole frontier for miles and counties will give way." In February 1863, Confederate Brigadier General William Hudson echoed Diamond's grim forecast on a visit to Montague County, thirty-six miles west of Gainesville. Hudson found locals greatly excited after numerous Indian depredations. Within a few weeks, continuing raids caused a wholesale panic among settlers. Residents abandoned many sections of Montague County along with all of Clay County to the west.[5]

Lt. Col. Buck Barry, the second highest ranking officer in the Texas Rangers during the war, recalled that the region's frontier counties "were almost entirely abandoned by the settlers" after the Elm Creek Raid in Young County in October 1864, with "only a few cowboys remaining at the large ranches—or as they were then called, 'forts.'" Confederate Col. John "Rip" Ford, who commanded Texas's Western District in 1864, observed, "The Texas frontier suffered greatly from Indian depredations during the war. A tier of counties, at least three deep, was quite depopulated."[6]

Citizens on the North Texas frontier also "forted up" in larger communities such as Montague, Gainesville, and Jacksboro. After the war, continuing raids and unsettled conditions during Reconstruction deterred residents from moving back to isolated rural areas for several years. Following the collapse of the Confederacy and the Texas state government, the Rangers disbanded. They would not reorganize until May 1874, as part of Major John B. Jones's Frontier Battalion. The U.S. Army did not send troops back to the North Texas frontier until the second half of 1866. During this period, residents of Montague, Cooke, and neighboring counties felt hopeless and abandoned.[7]

In September 1866, W. H. Whaley of Gainesville, Texas, wrote to the state's governor, J. W. Throckmorton, informing him that Cooke County settlers were in the direst situation since the county's founding in 1848. Devastating raids "of the most horrid character" by large groups of Indians and white outlaws threatened residents "almost daily." So many people in the upper portion of the county had abandoned their homesteads that "Gainesville might now be called an extreme [frontier] outpost." In one recent attack, marauders had killed and scalped two men near Gainesville and taken five hundred to six hundred head of horses.[8]

The letter noted that practically every community to the west and northwest of Gainesville was now deserted, and those who had not left the region were currently encamped close to the county seat. Whaley continued that it was "a pity that such a county as Cooke should be so necessitated to retrograde instead of advance in civilization and improvement." Area citizens proved no match for the number of depredations sweeping the county. "The raiders are as well armed as we are, each man bearing from one to two six-shooters besides guns and they fight equal to any white troops . . . They generally outnumber our men 2 or 3 to one."[9]

The following month, in October 1866, residents of Montague, Cooke, Denton, and Wise Counties sent a petition to Governor Throckmorton pleading for immediate relief against the incessant raids. The petition noted that the frontier line of settlement was rapidly receding eastward, and locals had determined that if they did not get some help within a few weeks, they would have no other option but to abandon their homes. Settlers in these North Texas counties reported that Indians were stealing all of their livestock. On September 30, 150 warriors passed through Cooke County, killing a man near Gainesville, wounding another, and making off with more than three hundred horses before heading west into Montague County. The September 30 incident came on the heels of another raid in Cooke County a few days earlier in which Indians murdered a man and took three women captive. The Comanches and Kiowas were reportedly "making such frequent raids in such large and formidable bodies that the citizens are in great terror."[10]

A year later, the situation had not improved. In October 1867, citizens of Montague County sent the new governor of Texas, E. M. Pease, a petition stating that throughout the fall warriors had been raiding Montague and adjacent counties, stealing livestock and "murdering and scalping or carrying into captivity women and children." In the preceding month and a half, Indians had repeatedly attacked the county seat of Montague and driven off large numbers of horses. The raiders brazenly passed through the county in daylight "without any effort to concealment." Desperate for some sort of assistance, locals complained to Pease that the U.S. Army outpost at Buffalo Springs, thirty miles west southwest of Montague, was too small and too far away to provide the requisite protection for area settlements.[11]

In a separate report, Montague County Judge F. W. Fanning informed the governor that between the second half of 1865 and February 1867, raiders had killed seven people, taken eight individuals captive, and stolen 191 horses. In addition, during this period, thieves had run off 11,625 head of cattle worth $124,670 from Montague County and neighboring Clay County. In adjacent Jack County, County Judge Thomas Williams reported that Indians had killed seven persons and taken one hundred horses and between one and five thousand head of cattle.[12]

To alleviate the chronic depredations, in July 1866 the federal government sent twenty-nine soldiers to Jacksboro, the county seat of Jack County. By the following month, the command had increased to sixty-two. As Jack County historian Allen Lee Hamilton notes, "That the troops had no immediate effect upon the security of the county probably came as no surprise to any citizens with appreciable frontier experience. . . . The raiding continued unabated." In late 1867 the army abandoned Buffalo Springs and started construction on a permanent post at Jacksboro named Fort Richardson. The fort was completed in 1870. For citizens of Montague County, the closest frontier garrisons were now at Fort Richardson in Jacksboro, 45 miles away, and at Fort Griffin in Shackelford County, 120 miles distant. Although the two federal outposts curtailed some of the Indian raiding, Comanche and Kiowa incursions into North Texas did not diminish until the end of the Red River War in June 1975, when the U.S. Army finally defeated these tribes and permanently relocated them to Indian Territory (now Oklahoma) north of the Red River.[13]

Besides widespread Indian depredations, assaults and murders by people of all ethnicities contributed to the pervasive violence in North Texas. Maintaining any semblance of law and order on the frontier proved a daunting task. Compounding the problem were anemic state and local law enforcement agencies and a fledgling criminal justice structure that had not yet firmly taken root. As a result, citizens had little faith that guilty parties would be apprehended, tried, convicted, and sent to prison through the legal system. Some settlers decided that their only recourse was to take the law into their own hands. One historian estimated that fifty-two vigilante groups were active in Texas, the most in the nation.[14]

Many communities lacked sufficient funds to pay constables and sheriffs to spend days or weeks out in the field tracking lawbreakers. Richard Maxwell Brown points out, "A really large expenditure for the pursuit, capture, jailing, trial, and conviction of culprits could easily bankrupt the typical frontier county or town." Compounding law enforcement challenges was a shortage of sturdy jails. The rickety, makeshift lockups in some frontier counties failed to deter prisoners from escaping. "Such deficiencies in the judicial system were the source of repeated complaints by frontiersmen . . . vigilantism was the solution to these problems."[15]

An apropos illustration is the Old Law Mob. From 1858 to 1861, this ruthless organization terrorized the North Texas frontier. These agitators preyed upon the local populace, incessantly stoking their fears while consistently positioning themselves as trusted, resolute leaders that anxious residents could turn to amidst the bedlam. The chaotic, unsettled state of the frontier perfectly suited the Mob's nefarious designs. The citizens were largely unaware that the demagogues were frequently manufacturing this chaos for their own advancement. Within a short time, mob members rose to leadership positions in North Texas militia units, making them very effective in cowing the populace.[16]

The Mob was a loose alliance of horse thieves, cutthroats, and opportunistic demagogues who intimidated the frontier populace to further their own ends.

The gang's activities included livestock rustling, arson, murder, and kidnapping. The chronic lawlessness they incited proved very effective in keeping locals on edge, silencing any opposition, and overwhelming the meager resources of Texas judges and sheriffs. Some Old Law Mob members posed as white knights, but their actions revealed them to be vicious, violent, and far from honest. These men were in league with the horse thieves as a marriage of convenience, one in which both parties got what they needed.[17]

Many frontier citizens were "compelled to remain quiet and swim with the current." In a confidential note to Texas Governor Sam Houston, Young County Surveyor James H. Swindells reported that a man could not speak out "without running the risk of being waylaid or dragged into a quarrel and shot down." Swindells told Houston, "We truly have a 'reign of terror' here." County officials were afraid to take action because they were unsure whom they could depend on for support; Swindells reported, "We do not know our enemies." In another appeal to the governor, R. W. Scott wrote from neighboring Cooke County, "The country is divided into factions and men are arrested and hung without law or trial, such things are horrible. The best man who has an enemy may be arrested by his influence and swept away from friends and family in an hour. Can nothing be done by the Governor?"[18]

Eventually, other vigilante committees in central Texas apprehended a number of Old Law Mob members. Although law enforcement officials tried to spare some of the prisoners who cooperated, locals ended up lynching them along with the others. Vigilantes refused to wait for lawmen and the Texas courts to take action against the Mob because getting indictments and successful convictions could take years, not to mention the problem of finding a secure jail to hold the prisoners. An illustrative jailbreak occurred in December 1858, when three accused rustlers escaped from the Young County Jail. One was recaptured after "a well contested foot race" with the jailer, but the other two got away. A newspaper report noted that even the best of jails could not contain these outlaws and, "This is the great reason why so many horse thieves have recently been lynched, as it was known [that] the jails would not hold them, and they would thus go unwhipt of justice."[19]

Although the grip of the Old Law Mob faded with the outbreak of the Civil War, vigilante activity on the North Texas frontier continued unabated during this era. In the Texas secession referendum held on February 23, 1861, the North Texas counties of Montague, Jack, Cooke, and Grayson all voted against disunion, four of nineteen Texas counties to do so. These counties strongly agreed with

Governor Sam Houston (1859–61) that secession would spell disaster for Texas, a prediction that proved all too true. Many local dissenters opposed Confederate military conscription and wanted to stay clear of the war.[20]

This prevailing sentiment set up a violent collision of sectional ideologies across North Texas as the North/Midwest/Upper South majority clashed with a radical fire-eater Lower South minority. For example, in Cooke County, 90 percent of the population did not own slaves, and many did not grow cotton. Despite the planters' minority status, they controlled 50 percent of the local economy. These slave owners, wielding their considerable wealth and political power along with a good measure of fear, intimidation, and violence, succeeded in suppressing the will of the majority.[21]

The North Texas anti-secession vote of 1861, in combination with the Texas Troubles of 1860 and John Brown's Raid in Virginia in 1859, created a dangerous and violent paranoia among the elite and their coterie. Slaveholders were now certain that slave-insurrection plots and abolitionist traitors were lurking around every corner. By 1862, the group had consolidated their political power and control over local military units. The South was at war, rumors swirled of a pending Union invasion of North Texas, and anyone who espoused anti-Confederate sentiments did so at their own peril.[22]

Matters came to a head in April 1862. On April 16, the Confederate Congress passed the Conscription Act, compelling mandatory military service in the Confederate Army. The announcement sparked widespread resentment and grumbling among citizens living in the Red River country and along the western frontier. Many of these residents had voted against secession and, like Sam Houston, had wanted Texas to stay in the Union. They held scant affection for the Confederacy and had no interest in serving in the Rebel army. They also had little use for rabble-rousing abolitionists. They wanted to be left alone on their farms where they could look after their families.[23]

Some of these disaffected citizens joined the Union League, also called the Peace Party, a clandestine group of locals determined to escape service in the Confederate Army. While the majority of Peace Party members did not advocate violent unrest against Rebel authorities, "a few" did. Within several months, the actions of this minority had sparked a lethal chain reaction, later known as the Great Hanging at Gainesville. During October 1862, Cooke County authorities, under District Provost Marshal James Bourland's direction, conducted a Peace Party witch hunt, arresting more than 150 suspected unionists and eventually hanging forty. Two others died attempting to escape. In Decatur, in neighboring

Wise County, authorities hung another five men allegedly affiliated with the Peace Party. The hangings did not quell dissent. Tensions over Rebel and Union loyalties continued to fester in North Texas. In the fall of 1864, Confederates surrounded the home of Jack County Sheriff Abner H. Hancock, a purported unionist. A shootout ensued in which Hancock and his wife died and their twenty-five-year-old son Leolan, a private in the Texas Rangers, was wounded.[24]

The Great Hanging at Gainesville and related regional violence graphically illustrate the consequences of mob hysteria taking hold of a community and residents temporarily taking leave of their senses, when law and order and due process crumble beneath the onslaught of lawless vigilantism. During the fall of 1862, area citizens descended into a dark pit of paranoia, and despite witnessing numerous extralegal actions against their neighbors by local authorities, took no action to stop them. As one member of the Great Hanging jury, Thomas Barrett, acknowledged "a good many innocent men were arrested" by Bourland's men. A reign of terror gripped the region. "Reason had left its throne. The mind of almost every man I saw seemed to be unhinged," Barrett recalled, "and wild excitement reigned supreme."[25]

Following the Civil War, the social order in Texas unraveled further. Barry Crouch and Donaly Brice note that during Reconstruction, "bandits 'infested' the highways and desperadoes roamed the countryside along with 'combinations of lawless men,' horse thieves, and other detestable characters . . . a 'spirit of lawlessness' reigned in Texas. The legal system had collapsed . . . citizens were intimidated in many areas." During this period, Texas had forty-five times more murders per year than the state of New York.[26]

The Civil War may have ended, but Confederate-Union tensions in North Texas continued to simmer. Unionists wanted atonement for the Great Hanging and other Rebel lynchings in the region. Former Confederates fiercely resisted. In the summer of 1865, a mob affiliated with the Union League was thwarted in its attempt to lynch Wise County Sheriff Robert Cates, who had hung the five men in Decatur during the Great Hanging panic. In nearby Cooke County, authorities indicted fourteen of the principal leaders responsible for the Great Hanging. A number of these, including James Bourland, threatened armed resistance. The district judge, William Thomas Green Weaver, was alleged to have "deliberately issued faulty arrest writs" that were delivered too late, allowing some of the indicted to escape. Finally, in the fall of 1866, six of those involved in the hangings were tried in Weaver's Gainesville court. Cooke County juries acquitted all six. Sensing an opening, former Confederates in North Texas implemented a vigorous and effective campaign of intimidation and violence to squelch efforts at prosecuting wartime crimes. In one instance, ex-Rebel vigilantes dressed up as raiding Indians to terrorize unionists. In the end, area unionists never received the justice and retribution they felt they deserved for wrongs committed against them during the war and its aftermath.[27]

Compounding this swirling chaos were unresolved civil and judicial problems related to Reconstruction that hampered the restoration of city and county governments. An excellent illustration is District Judge Weaver's circuit tour of North Texas in the spring of 1867. During his rounds to the various courts within his district, Weaver dealt with raiding Indians and vigilante mobs that had been terrorizing the region. In his report to Governor J. W. Throckmorton, Weaver stated that he had journeyed first to Jack County, where he found the local government "almost disorganized." Nonetheless, the judge managed to convene a grand jury. Weaver then held court "on the subject of mobs and the crime of murder and instructed [the grand jury] to indict all those who had participated in the various outrages private and mobocratic [sic] committed during the war." In 1861 Jack County citizens had voted overwhelmingly against secession. Weaver discovered that there was considerable divergence of opinion between former Confederate and Union sympathizers in the county regarding wartime vigilantism.[28]

On the way to his next stop in Decatur in Wise County, Weaver found the area "full of Indians. . . . All the country was in a state of Alarm—I had no [armed military] escort—The Indians came down and returned by the Jacksboro Road in open day." Following this incursion, the judge felt it would be unwise to continue the court session. Moreover, he found scant semblance of government in Wise County, which still lacked a county court and a district clerk. Furthermore, the judge observed that "no competent men can be got to hold office."[29]

Weaver next rode to Montague County, where he encountered depressingly similar problems. He was able to organize a grand jury but could not convene a petit jury. The judge spent two days "in fruitless efforts to make a jury . . . it was deemed useless . . . to make further effort—Court will adjourn today." Closing his report to the governor, Judge Weaver said, "I still hope for better times after Reconstruction."[30]

In his report, Weaver mentioned not having an armed military escort, something that a number of Texas jurists insisted upon during this period. Judge Moses B. Walker of the Fourth Judicial District, Judge B. F. Barkley of Fort Worth, and Judge Hardin Hart of the Seventh Judicial District (Weaver's successor) all had soldiers guarding them. During one of the England family murder trials in 1876, a detachment of Texas Rangers guarded District Judge J. A. Carroll's Montague courtroom. Judges and courtrooms were vulnerable not only to Indian raids but also to vigilantes who opposed judicial proceedings or verdicts. Lawless mobs frequently circumvented North Texas's nascent criminal justice system.[31]

Robert DeArment wrote, "Gangs of horse thieves and cattle rustlers ran rampant throughout the frontier counties of northern Texas." County sheriffs, tasked with covering an enormous area despite limited resources were "outnumbered and outgunned, . . . simply incapable of controlling the criminals." Because local law enforcement could not stem the tide, residents took matters into their own hands and formed several vigilante groups. The most famous of these was the Vigilance Committee, or Tin-Hat Brigade, in the Fort Griffin/Shackelford County area, 120 miles southwest of Montague. Starting in 1876, the Vigilance Committee, up to 150 members strong, actively confronted outlaws and within two years had driven all alleged lawbreakers from the region. In perhaps its best known act, on June 24, 1878, ten to twenty members of the group donned masks, entered the Shackelford County Jail, and gunned down former sheriff John Larn, who had long been suspected of livestock rustling. Larn died of nine gunshot wounds.[32]

During Reconstruction, Montague County had its own vigilance committee, the Law and Order League. This vigilante group was formed in 1872 at Red River Station, northwest of Nocona, Texas. Locals had become fed up because an influx of "the worst characters" from Indian Territory and the Texas frontier were rendezvousing in the county. A Major Bronson was reportedly the leader of the league, which had "beats" in every precinct, each beat commanded by a captain.[33]

The Law and Order League's stated purpose was to help local authorities in apprehending horse and cattle thieves and "other bad characters" who were crossing the Red River and terrorizing Montague County settlers. Typically, the vigilantes would turn over any outlaws they caught to county officials for prosecution. Near the end of 1873, however, some members of the Law and Order League began taking the law into their own hands, becoming judge, jury, and executioner. Rather than have the county attorney or sheriff take charge of their prisoners, these vigilantes started hanging or shooting the men they detained. By 1876, members of the group had purportedly killed fourteen people in Montague County.[34]

The Law and Order League started unraveling in the spring of 1876, when one member, Sampson Barras, went to Montague County Attorney Avery Matlock and gave evidence against his brothers-in-law, George and Andrew Brown. Brown family members were captains of "Brown's Beat," the league's precinct at Farmers

Creek, southeast of Spanish Fort, Texas. Barras told Matlock that George and
Andrew, along with their brother Jesse and father George Sr., had committed a
number of murders. Barras served as head of the vigilante group's "lynch party."[35]

In exchange for a reduced sentence, Barras implicated the Browns and their
associates in the killing of Robert "Rat" Morrow in 1873. Members of Brown's
Beat riddled Morrow with several shotgun blasts outside his Farmers Creek home
and finished him off with a pistol shot to the throat. Two years later, the gang
went after Morrow's widow, Elizabeth, who had moved to Saint Jo. In June 1875,
at ten o'clock at night, a group of men fired seven bullets through her bedroom
window. Elizabeth Morrow fled outside, where the waiting vigilantes gunned
her down in the yard.[36]

In another assault in November 1875 on the Red River, affiliates of Brown's
Beat waylaid one of their own, Freeman Batchlor, a resident of Farmers Creek.
Apparently, the killing was sparked by an intergang rivalry for the affections of a
"buxom lass of seventeen." After shooting Batchlor, the vigilantes robbed him and
severed his head. A fourth incident involving Brown's crew occurred in May 1876,
when the Brown brothers ambushed Doc McClain on Farmers Creek. Sampson
Barras and his brother John participated in the slaying. McClain's murder was
the fourteenth and final homicide attributed to the league. Barras's testimony
proved crucial in convicting George and Andrew Brown. By the summer of 1876,
Montague County's Law and Order League was dismantled.[37]

Commenting on the flurry of vigilante activity in North Texas, area newspaper
editors acknowledged that while vigilantism was normally not the preferred option
in a law-abiding society, out on the frontier the weak law enforcement and court
systems left locals with no other recourse. The only things that deterred horse
thieves and cattle rustlers were "blue whistlers [bullets] or hemp [rope]." Peaceable
residents who had stomached enough chaos and lawlessness were determined
to rid the country of outlaw vermin, come what may. G. W. Robson, editor of
the *Jacksboro Frontier Echo*, pointed out to readers that in "no instance is [it] yet
recorded where the law has paid the slightest attention to lynchers of this kind.
It is conceded by judge and jury that the man who steals a horse in Texas forfeits
his life to the owner."[38]

There have been no detailed studies of lynching and criminal justice in North
Texas during this period, but William Carrigan's work on central Texas offers
some excellent parallels. Carrigan found a direct correlation between increases in
competency of local courts and citizens' trust in the legal process, and a decrease
in lynching. Prior to 1890, 68 percent of all grand jury murder indictments never

went to trial—often because sheriffs and constables were unable to locate indicted suspects or the witnesses against them.[39]

As Texas legal historian Michael Ariens notes, "Violent crime in Texas, including murder, was rampant in the 1870s, and the clearance rate was quite low. That helps explain the rise of vigilance committees." Because of the "extraordinary instability" during this period and the dearth of law and order, the public had little faith in the Texas legal system. Even in large cities such as Dallas, residents expressed frustration. In September 1875, the *Dallas Weekly Herald* reported, "The people—the bone and sinew of the country—are losing confidence in the courts and justice. This leads to mob violence and lynch law."[40]

In a before-and-after comparison, Carrigan documents criminal justice improvements in central Texas in the years following Reconstruction. He found that the bleak state of law and order in the region improved significantly after 1890. By that date two-thirds of all grand jury indictments went to trial. The conviction rate also rose to almost 60 percent, and juries more often meted out harsh sentences, including death penalties and life sentences.[41]

In sum, Carrigan found that after 1890, several significant changes were taking root: More cases went to trial, juries convicted more lawbreakers, the sentences were longer, and more criminals were sent to the state penitentiary. Taken together, "these changes undermined the intellectual defense of mob violence [that many had previously used]. The charge of an ineffective legal system no longer had the same resonance." Once again, Carrigan's conclusions regarding central Texas during this period are applicable to North Texas.[42]

Following Reconstruction, the nature of lynching changed in the Lone Star State. By 1900, the lynching of whites in Texas was uncommon. Lynchings were now predominately race-related and utilized as a means of intimidating African Americans and Hispanics. Although the state's criminal justice system had made significant strides, in cases involving blacks or Mexican Americans, citizens often insisted on taking the law into their own hands. In 1891, authorities hung twenty-seven people convicted of murder while, by comparison, vigilantes lynched 140 Texans.[43]

Lynchings, lawlessness, vigilantism, and a weak legal system. This was the social backdrop of North Texas's postbellum period against which the England murder case played out. With this background now in place, I turn to the story of Ben Krebs.

$$= 3 =$$

Many people never could get Ben Krebs's name or nationality right. Some spelled his last name Cribs or Cribbs, others as Kribs or Kribbs. He was also often called a "Dutchman," nineteenth-century American slang for someone from Germany, Austria, Switzerland, Belgium, or the Netherlands. In fact, Ben was born in Switzerland in 1828 and immigrated to the United States in 1850. By October of that year, he had become an American citizen and was living in western Wisconsin. Seven years later, in 1857, Krebs moved to Young County, Texas. Upon arriving there, he purchased a town lot in the county seat of Belknap. Krebs was a man of modest means who worked as a laborer and farmer to make ends meet. Besides the town lot and a horse, he had little to his name.[1]

By June 1860, Krebs was employed by the Overland Mail Company as a stage driver based in western Young County, near present-day Proffitt, Texas. From 1858 to 1861, the Overland Mail Company had a $600,000 annual contract with the United States Postmaster General to transport mail and passengers from Saint Louis and Memphis to San Francisco. One-quarter of the 2,800-mile transcontinental route, known as the Butterfield Overland Mail Line (after company president John Butterfield), ran through Texas. The manager of the Butterfield station where Krebs lived was William A. George of Indiana. George, his wife, Mary, and their two children shared living quarters with Krebs and another Butterfield stagecoach driver, L. B. Carlille of New York. Although George was in charge of day-to-day operations, over time the stage stop acquired the name Cribbs's Station, after Ben Krebs.[2]

Cribbs's Station was not on the original Butterfield Mail Line itinerary for 1858. In fine-tuning the mail route and shortening the distance between stage stops during November 1858, the Overland Mail Company added a new relay point halfway between Belknap Station and Frans's Station, twenty miles apart. The mail company built a log cabin near a large waterhole on a creek (later dubbed Cribb Station Creek), eleven miles west southwest of Belknap. In her history of Young County, Texas, Carrie Crouch notes that "Cribb Station was the first stop west of Belknap on the Butterfield Overland Mail Route where Ben Cribb ran the stable and a store in the pre-war days."[3]

With the coming of the Civil War, the Butterfield route was abandoned and the federal army withdrew from Texas. The isolated and exposed location of Cribbs's Station motivated its inhabitants to move elsewhere for safety. Ben Krebs stayed in Young County through 1862, but by 1864 had relocated to Montague County. From February through June 1864, Cpl. Ben Krebs served in Capt. Sevier Shannon's Company B from Montague County, part of the Twenty-First Brigade of the Texas State Troops, assigned to protect the First Frontier District.[4]

In the following year, 1865, Krebs married Eliza Ann "Rhoda" Taylor Savage, whose first husband, Wiley Blount Savage had died the previous year. Wiley and Rhoda Savage had had two children during their eight-year marriage, Mary Jane and Johnnie Savage. After their wedding, Ben, Rhoda, Mary Jane, and Johnnie lived in a log cabin in Montague, the county seat of Montague County. By 1866, Ben and Rhoda had welcomed their first child together, William.[5]

One of the Krebs family's nearest neighbors was Rhoda's stepson, Thomas N. Savage, a son from Wiley Blount Savage's first marriage. Rhoda's mother and father, Jane Barnett Taylor and William Hampton Taylor, also lived nearby with two of their children, Aaron Kendrick Taylor and William Barnett "Bill" Taylor. William Hampton Taylor, a blacksmith and farmer, had a reputation as "a heavy drinker. He would often get drunk and go home and curse and abuse his family." A frequent target of his physical violence was his fifteen-year-old son Bill.[6]

Late in the evening of January 29, 1869, a frightened Bill Taylor showed up on his sister's doorstep. Rhoda and Ben Krebs were already in bed. Ben got up, opened the door, and asked Bill what the matter was. The distressed teenager rushed into the Krebs home with a pistol in hand. Apparently, his father was drunk and in a violent temper. William Taylor had threatened Bill, saying that he was going to whip him. Bill told Ben that he was fed up with being beaten by his father and was leaving home. Bill planned to collect his clothes and horse the next day. Until then he needed a safe place to lie down and get some rest. Rhoda made a bed for him on the floor and the household settled down to sleep.[7]

In the meantime, the inebriated and belligerent William Taylor had been scouring the neighborhood for Bill. First, he went to the home of Thomas Savage. Taylor pounded on the door, demanding to know if his son was inside. Savage opened the door and replied that Bill was not there. Savage noticed that William Taylor was carrying a holstered pistol strapped to his waist. Taylor admonished him, "Tom, don't tell me a lie." Savage repeated that he had no idea where Bill was. Taylor stormed off saying, "I'll whip him to death if I can find him."[8]

Taylor went next to the Krebs home and beat on the door, demanding to know if Bill was inside. Rhoda told him that his son was not there. Taylor again shouted through the door, this time asking Ben Krebs if Bill was inside. Taylor threatened Ben, "Don't tell me a lie or I will shoot you." Then, inexplicably, Ben contradicted his wife and acknowledged that Bill was in their home. Ben opened the door and William Taylor barged in, with the pistol in his belt and a switch in his hand, ranting, "I am going to get him out of here or I will whip him out of here."[9]

A shot rang out from the interior of the house and William Taylor cried out, "I am killed." Ben propped him up against the door to keep him from falling and helped take off his coat to examine the wound. He had been shot through the chest. Taylor said to his son, "See, Bill, what you have done? Now you've killed me." Bill, sitting on his bed, replied, "Yes, you have abused me, and you came here to abuse me again." The teen got up and walked out. Ben Krebs then helped William Taylor to lie down. Within five minutes, Taylor was dead. In the meantime, young Bill, pistol still in hand, went to Thomas Savage's home and told Savage, "Tom, I have shot Pap." Savage told him, "Billy, I would never have done that, I would do anything before shooting my father." Bill Taylor replied, "I couldn't help it."[10]

Ben Krebs recalled that following the killing, Montague County officials made no effort to arrest young Bill for his father's murder, a stark example of the ineffectiveness of local law enforcement during Reconstruction. Finally, on February 8, 1869, someone notified the nearest federal authority at Fort Richardson in Jacksboro, Texas, of the murder. The following day, post commander Maj. Robert Murray Morris of the Sixth Cavalry ordered a detail of eight men under the command of Lt. W. A. Borthwick to proceed to Montague and arrest Bill Taylor. On February 14, Borthwick and his squad brought Taylor back to Jacksboro in irons and placed him in the post jail. On May 24, a grand jury in

Montague indicted Bill Taylor for murder, and he remained in custody until the end of May, when District Judge Hardin Hart released him on $10,000 bail.[11]

Writing to his superiors, the new commander at Fort Richardson, Col. James Oakes, expressed surprise that a judge would allow bail for an indicted murder suspect. E. B. Turner, the attorney for civil affairs at the Attorney General's Office in Austin, told Oakes it was only in capital murder cases that bail was automatically refused. In each instance, it was up to the presiding judge to determine whether there was sufficient evidence for a capital murder charge and to rule on bail accordingly. Judge Hart defended his bail decision to Oakes, explaining that during the district court's regular rotation, only one week was allotted to hold court at Montague, which was not enough time to put Bill Taylor on trial. Hart, like other district judges in Texas, traveled a circuit, holding court in the county seats within his district. In addition, Hart pointed out that he had only two noncommissioned officers and privates to guard his Montague court while in session, and he did not deem that force sufficient to protect prisoners in custody. The unsettled nature of the North Texas frontier meant that isolated district courts such as Hardin Hart's required a strong military guard to ensure they could function safely.[12]

Authorities eventually put Bill Taylor on trial in Montague for murdering his father, where he was represented by Gainesville attorney Dick Burdough. A jury acquitted Bill and he returned home, where in July 1870, he was living with his widowed mother, Jane, and his brother Aaron. Reflecting upon his father's death, Bill likely resented his brother-in-law Ben and perhaps also his sister Rhoda for what had happened. Why would Ben tell William Taylor that Bill was in the Krebs home after Rhoda said he was not? And why would Ben then let the drunken and abusive Taylor inside? Ben's actions put Bill in direct danger of bodily harm. The teenager felt trapped, left with no other recourse but to defend himself from his violent father who had physically abused him on a number of previous occasions. After Bill Taylor killed his father, the trajectory of his life took a decided turn for the worse. Following a brief three-month stint as a private in the Texas Rangers from late 1873 to early 1874, he left home and began committing crimes in North Texas and Indian Territory with a gang of outlaws.[13]

On July 4, 1874, a few months after concluding his frontier service with the Rangers, Bill stole a gelding. On March 17, 1875, Montague County officials indicted him for horse theft, and he began living a life "on the dodge." Soon, Montague County Sheriff Lee Perkins had arrest warrants for Bill Taylor on several charges.

A Texas Ranger fugitive report described Bill as 5 feet, 8 inches to 5 feet, 10 inches in height, weighing 140–150 pounds. The report noted that Taylor "drinks and gambles a good deal, [and] is very profane and vulgar." Another account characterized him as "an escaped convict and a refugee from justice."[14]

A year after William Taylor's murder, Rhoda and Ben Krebs welcomed their second child, Georgia Ann "Annie" Krebs. Around this time, the Krebs family relocated six miles south of Montague to the 160-acre Wiley B. Savage Survey. Rhoda had inherited the land after the death of her first husband, Wiley. Their property and those of their nearest neighbors bordered Denton Creek and lay along the road from Montague to Decatur, Texas. Ben and Rhoda owned twenty-five head of cattle, two horses, and a town lot in the county seat of Montague, for a total net worth of $890. Locals in Montague County viewed Ben Krebs as a truthful, upstanding citizen, as evidenced by his service in the Texas State Troops, as a juror on the County Police Court, and as Montague County District Clerk.[15]

Ben and Rhoda were close with their neighbors, many of whom were relatives. A 160-acre property to the northeast was owned by Rhoda's stepson, Thomas N. Savage, their neighbor in Montague. To the southeast was the William Hampton Taylor survey, also 160 acres, which Rhoda's father had owned. When William Taylor surveyed his land in September 1856, Rhoda's first husband, Wiley Savage, assisted as a chain carrier.[16]

In the years following William Taylor's murder, the composition of the Taylor-Savage-Krebs neighborhood began to change. Bill Taylor fled home and became a fugitive, while Thomas Savage sold his property. By 1875, Selena England of Whitesboro, Texas, had purchased the 160-acre Thomas N. Savage Survey. The Englands' home near Denton Creek was situated a half mile northeast of Ben and Rhoda Krebs's cabin. Selena and William England built a fine home on the property for their family, which included several children from Selena's previous marriage, Isaiah, Harvey, and Susie Taylor. Selena's first husband, Billington J. Taylor (no relation to William Taylor), was a farmer and blacksmith who died in Whitesboro in 1866 or 1867. Her next-door-neighbor at the time was Rev. William England, a Methodist minister. England's first wife, Chloe, passed away in September 1870. Although England was twenty-six years older than Selena, a courtship ensued and on December 7, 1870, the two were married.[17]

Another neighbor of the Englands' was the John and Luna Music family, who also lived a half mile distant. The Musics had recently settled in Montague County, where John had lived as a child. John R. Music was born in Arkansas in 1849, the son of William Granville Music and Louisa Perkins Music. In 1850, William and

Louisa Music were living in Mill Creek Township, Franklin County, Arkansas. During the 1850s, William and Louisa divorced. By 1856 Louisa had remarried, to Hiram Gibson, with whom she had three children. In 1860 Louisa and Hiram Gibson were living near Webb City, Franklin County, Arkansas.[18]

After the divorce from Louisa, William Music moved to North Texas with his son John. In October 1858, twenty-eight-year-old William G. Music enlisted at Gainesville, Texas, as a private in Texas Ranger Capt. James Bourland's company of mounted volunteers. (Bourland later oversaw the Great Hanging at Gainesville in 1862.) In April 1859, Bourland discharged William Music from his Ranger company for disobedience of orders. The following year, in 1860, William was living in Montague County, Texas, with a new wife, eighteen-year-old Elizabeth, and his son John. In 1863, William had 160 acres, 1 horse, 22 cattle, and 63 sheep. In February 1864, Pvt. William G. Music enlisted at Montague, Texas, in Capt. J. P. Guinn's Company of the Texas State Troops, First Frontier District, commanded by Maj. William Quayle. In early 1864, William's wife, Elizabeth Music, was one of twelve women "forted up" in Montague, Texas, who implored state officials for armed protection while their husbands were away on military service. On May 15, 1864, William Music deserted his company (and likely his family) and was officially designated as AWOL.[19]

William and Louisa Music's son, John, seemed restless and moved frequently throughout his life. In 1869, John was working as a blacksmith in Hunt County, Texas, where he met Luna Broderick Smith. Luna was born in Washington County, Illinois, in 1849, the daughter of William Daniel Bohning Smith and Rebecca Minerva Bird. On March 6, 1869, Luna married John Music. After a little more than two years of marriage, they divorced. Luna then married James W. Harris on August 15, 1872, in Hunt County, Texas, but the union did not last. By 1874, Luna and John were back together, and Luna gave birth to their second daughter, Louisa Belle, in Pilot Point, Texas. In 1876 John Music decided to return to Montague County. John, Luna, and their two children moved into a home bordering the T. N. Savage Survey.[20]

Interestingly, in 1860, Music's father, William Granville Music, had intended to homestead the Savage property that Selena England purchased fifteen years later. William Music surveyed the land in October 1860 but failed to live there for three consecutive years as required by Texas homestead law. By 1868, the State of Texas considered the land vacant and Thomas Savage settled on it. In 1871, after Savage homesteaded the acreage, the Texas General Land Office issued him a patented title to the 160 acres.[21]

In June 1876, John Music ran afoul of Montague County authorities when he was indicted for the theft of a steer. In a display of neighborly solidarity, Thomas Savage, Ben Krebs, and Krebs's friend and former neighbor, James Preston, each pitched in $300 to cover Music's bond. When the county attorney brought the case to trial, a jury of six men acquitted Music of the cattle rustling charge and ordered him released without delay. A month later, in July 1876, Ben Krebs had his own brush with the law when William and Selena England filed aggravated assault charges against him. Prior to this incident, the Krebs and England families had been on good terms.[22]

The dispute centered on the Englands' livestock, which kept getting into Krebs's cornfield and ruining his crop. On July 26, 1876, the Englands lodged a formal complaint against Krebs, who immediately hired Montague attorney William H. Grigsby to represent him. Grigsby told his client that he had a good chance of beating the aggravated assault charge, but if found guilty, the punishment was a $100 to $1,000 fine and up to two years in jail. Montague County Court officials scheduled a hearing on the England-Krebs dispute for Monday, September 4, 1876.[23]

During the month of August 1876, Krebs met with his lawyer to discuss the pending assault trial. Krebs said he had several witnesses willing to testify on his behalf. Grigsby asked him to bring them to his law office in Montague on Saturday, August 26, 1876. Krebs was prepared to do this when one or several of the witnesses said they had a schedule conflict and could not meet that day. As it turned out, the murder of the England family on August 26 made the September 4 hearing unnecessary.[24]

Two months after the slayings, on Halloween 1876, the Montague County grand jury indicted Ben Krebs, James Preston, and Aaron Kendrick Taylor for the England murders. On the same day, the Montague County District Court ordered Sheriff Lee Perkins to summon sixty good and lawful men as potential jurors. On November 3, authorities brought the prisoners to district court, where all three entered pleas of not guilty. After recording their pleas, Sixteenth Judicial District Judge Joseph Alexander Carroll directed that they be returned to jail to await trial. On November 7, the court granted Aaron Taylor a continuance and on November 9 did the same for James Preston. In Ben Krebs's case, however, Judge Carroll denied a motion for continuance and ordered an immediate trial. Reporting on the legal proceedings, the *Galveston Daily News* described Krebs as the "dastardly leader" of the murderous plot.[25]

On November 10, 1876, Montague County put Ben Krebs on trial for the England murders. The Montague legal firm of William H. Grigsby and Frank Willis represented Krebs, while District Attorney Finis E. Piner was prosecutor for the State of Texas, and County Attorney Avery Lenoir Matlock was prosecutor for Montague County. Judge Carroll was presiding judge.[26]

The respective attorneys impaneled a jury and the Krebs trial got underway. Three witnesses for the prosecution, Harvey Taylor, Jonathan Stroud, and W. Y. Nix were ready to testify that they heard Krebs threaten bodily harm to various members of the England family during July and August 1876. Krebs's counsel objected to Harvey Taylor's testimony as hearsay, arguing that Harvey could only testify that there had been a difficulty between Krebs and the Englands but could not provide specific details of the confrontation. Judge Carroll overruled the objection.[27]

Harvey Taylor testified that in July 1876, he, Selena, and William England were repairing a fence to keep their family's hogs out of Krebs's cornfield. Harvey stated that while they were there, they heard the sounds of dogs barking and hogs squealing. Shortly thereafter, Ben Krebs appeared on his side of the fence and the Englands showed him several cracks in the boards where the swine had been slipping through. Krebs, obviously frustrated, picked up a six-foot fence stake and raised it in an angry and threatening manner several times at the elderly Reverend England. Selena England interposed and told Krebs to talk to her. Harvey stated that Krebs lifted the stake again and replied, "God damn you, if you come down here anymore, I will kill you." Krebs then went with Harvey Taylor to nearby Denton Creek, where they had a long talk. Harvey recalled that Krebs told him that he had nothing against him personally, but regarding Harvey's stepfather he said, "If William England is a Christian and does [his neighbors] this way, I have no use for Christianity—hell is broiling for such men as he is."[28]

Krebs's lawyers also objected to the testimony of the next witness, Jonathan Stroud. Judge Carroll overruled this motion as well. Stroud recalled that during July 1876 he was passing along the road that ran near the Krebs home when he ran into Harvey Taylor's brother, Isaiah, and another man named Bridgewater. While they were conversing, Ben and Rhoda Krebs walked up to the three men. Isaiah Taylor and Bridgewater then continued on together, while Stroud began conversing with the Krebses about a thresher. According to Stroud, Ben switched topics and started talking about his recent confrontation with the England family. Stroud claimed that Krebs pointed his finger at Isaiah Taylor and said, "If I ever get a chance at that damned rascal, [I] will clean him up." Stroud said that Krebs was upset over the Englands' encroaching livestock and their continuing damage to his crops, and that "he had been run over about as long as he intended to allow."[29]

After Stroud concluded his testimony, W. Y. Nix gave evidence that in the first part of August 1876, Krebs had stopped by Hammond's Blacksmith Shop in Montague to visit with John Music, Nix, and proprietor Albert Hammond, who was shoeing a horse. Nix recalled that Krebs, who was standing about four or five feet from him, was fuming about the Englands' assault allegation. Krebs, obviously agitated, demonstrated to those gathered exactly what had happened during his altercation with Selena and her husband. Krebs said that because of them he had been indicted for assault, and that "before he would be sent to the penitentiary, he would kill the England family."[30]

C. G. McGuire followed Nix in the witness box. McGuire stated that on the morning after the murders, Sunday, August 27, he had gone to the England home and joined the crowd of curious onlookers gathered there. He was sitting on a woodpile when he noticed Ben Krebs and James Preston coming up the road from Krebs's home. McGuire said that as the two men passed close to him, "he observed that they were both very pale and were trembling so much that he could see their clothes shake on them."[31]

Taking the stand after McGuire, Dr. J. E. Stinson stated that at the behest of county authorities, he and three others had conducted a search of the Krebs home on the morning of Monday, August 28. Upon entering the cabin, Stinson assured Rhoda Krebs that nothing would be disturbed. One item Stinson was looking for was a shirt belonging to Ben Krebs. When the doctor had observed Krebs among the crowd gathered at the England home on Sunday morning, he noticed Krebs was wearing a fresh, clean shirt. Stinson wanted to know the whereabouts of the clothing that Krebs had worn on Saturday night and asked Rhoda to produce it. Krebs's wife was unable to find it, but her daughter, fifteen-year-old Mary Jane Savage, located the worn article in the attic. The shirt was tightly rolled up and had bloodstains on it. Stinson said that Rhoda and her children seemed taken aback by the bloodied garment. The doctor could not determine if the blood was human or animal. Forensic science, including blood type analysis and ballistics testing, was unknown on the Texas frontier in 1876.[32]

Continuing his testimony, Stinson said that after Mary Jane found the shirt, Rhoda told him that her husband had changed his clothing on Saturday morning, August 26, before going to Montague with her. She had insisted to Ben that if he went to town with her, he must wear a clean shirt and look presentable. Taking possession of Krebs's bloodstained garment, Stinson asked Rhoda if there were any firearms in her home. She replied that there was only an old rusty, broken pistol, which she showed them. A short time later, however, the doctor and his assistants found a Colt Navy Revolver. The revolver had five fresh rounds in it, while the sixth barrel was empty and had recently been fired.[33]

Stinson came across this six-shooter hidden among some clothes in a cupboard. Once again, Rhoda Krebs expressed surprise at the discovery. She claimed that someone had placed it there several months previously and that it had not been used for a considerable time. During his search, Stinson and his group also discovered eight or nine lead pistol balls (bullets) in the Krebs home that appeared to be a perfect fit for the Colt Navy Revolver. The doctor noted that these bullets were of the same caliber as two pistol balls he had recovered from the room where William England was killed.[34]

Testifying for the defense, Rhoda Krebs gave a muddled account while attempting to clarify the doctor's statements. With regard to the rolled-up shirt in the attic, Rhoda recalled that on Friday, August 25, the day before the murders, Ben had killed and cleaned two turkeys. He had cut their necks, skinned and gutted them, then hung them on the stable door. She stated that she could not remember if her husband had gotten any blood on his clothing while butchering the turkeys.[35]

Rhoda's explanation for the Colt Navy Revolver that Stinson found was garbled and thoroughly confusing. She claimed she didn't know there were two pistols in the house because she had forgotten about the revolver being in the cupboard. Rhoda recalled that she had told her thirteen-year-old son, Johnnie Savage, to place the revolver in a safe place where it would not go off by accident. She did not see where the teen put the gun. Then under cross-examination, she contradicted her previous testimony, claiming that on Saturday her brother Aaron Taylor had put the pistol in the cupboard by the door, where it was later found by Dr. Stinson. Rhoda said that the revolver belonged to her son, Johnnie, who had loaded it the day before the murders. Aaron Taylor had subsequently shot one round from it while hunting turkeys. After Aaron returned, she told him to put the gun in a safe place so that it would not fall to the floor and accidently discharge.[36]

Rhoda also said that Mary Jane had gone out into the yard while Stinson was searching the house, located Ben Krebs's shirt there, and handed it to the doctor. Mary Jane Savage, who gave evidence after Rhoda, confirmed her mother's story that Ben had changed shirts on Saturday after cleaning the turkeys, and stated she had seen him go to bed wearing the same clean shirt on Saturday night.[37]

Mary Jane then refuted both Dr. Stinson's and Rhoda's statements that she was the one who found the bloodstained shirt. Mary Jane said her mother asked her to go out to the bin where the family put their dirty clothes and search for Ben's soiled shirt. She was unable to find the garment but someone else eventually found it in the attic. Mary Jane was certain that she had not put the shirt in the attic, nor had she given it to the doctor. In the end, exactly who found the blood-spattered clothing and where it was found was never clearly established.[38]

After Mary Jane left the witness stand, her brother Johnnie told the court that the Colt Navy Revolver found by Stinson belonged to him. Savage said that he had traded a hog for the pistol a few weeks before the killings. He had loaded the firearm on Friday. The following day, Rhoda's brother, Aaron Taylor, had fired one round from it while out hunting turkeys. Johnnie also corroborated Rhoda's and Mary Jane's evidence regarding Ben Krebs having changed into a clean shirt on Saturday prior to going into Montague. Johnnie had accompanied his mother and stepfather to town that day.[39]

Defense witnesses Gus White and Louis Fisch then testified that they had ridden into Montague in a wagon with the Krebs family on Saturday and that Ben was wearing a clean shirt. After White and Fisch concluded their remarks, local resident Andy Patrick stated that he had lunched with Ben and Rhoda in Montague on Saturday and that Ben's shirt was freshly washed. Prosecution witness D. D. White took the stand next and rebutted White, Fisch, and Patrick, claiming that when he saw Ben Krebs in Montague that Saturday, he had on a soiled shirt that looked very much like the bloodstained garment Stinson removed from the Krebs home.[40]

During her testimony, Rhoda Krebs also described events at the Krebs household on August 26, the night of the murders. Rhoda recalled that when she and Ben returned from Montague on Saturday afternoon, their friend and former neighbor James Preston was at their house. Preston had been bunking with the Krebs family for several days while tending crops on his adjacent property. Just before sunset, he announced that he was leaving for his home at Sandy, eighteen miles distant. The Krebs invited him to stay for dinner and spend the night. Preston accepted the invitation. Joining them for supper was Rhoda's brother, Aaron Taylor, who was also sleeping over.[41]

Rhoda prepared dinner and after the meal was eaten, they all sat for a while and visited. Outside the wolves were howling, and Ben remarked that this often happened when Indians were in the neighborhood. The group discussed Indians until about an hour after sunset, at approximately nine o'clock, when everyone called it a night. Aaron Taylor said that he wanted sleep out in the yard where it was a little cooler. Ben told him to stay in the house, lest he catch cold sleeping outside. Rhoda made beds for everyone on the floor. She and Mary Jane slept in one bed, Ben and James Preston in another, and Aaron Taylor and Johnnie Savage in a third. The household dropped off to sleep for two or three hours before being awakened by loud noises sometime between eleven and midnight.[42]

Ben Krebs exclaimed, "What in the name of God does that mean?" James Preston sprang up from his bed and started for the door to investigate. Ben told him to stay inside because there could be raiding Indians nearby. After getting dressed, Ben, Rhoda, Aaron, and Preston stepped outside to listen. Preston wondered, "if it was Indians, robbers, or someone drunk up at the pond, near old man England's." Rhoda said that she had heard gunfire in her sleep and then once awake, had heard three more gunshots."[43]

The group stayed outside for about thirty minutes, listening to the eerie, frightening sounds drifting across the field toward their house. They thought they "heard a woman screaming, but the . . . [dog] was barking at old man England's, and the wolves howling," so they could not be sure what was going on. Preston wondered if someone had been killed. When the group came back inside, they were shaken, terrified that the Comanches were out on a rampage slaughtering their neighbors. Johnnie Savage recalled that the moon was almost down when they finally turned in for the night. The next morning, Rhoda's stepson Tom Savage stopped by to tell them of the grisly murders at the England home.[44]

The next person to give evidence was Harvey Taylor, the only living survivor of the August 26 carnage. In his initial testimony, Harvey said that the two men who had been crouching by the England's front gate were large in stature, "about the size of Ben Krebs and James Preston." Harvey did not, however, specifically identify Krebs and Preston as the two men. When recalled later for additional testimony, he undercut the prosecution's case, casting doubt on Ben Krebs's participation in the carnage. In her deathbed statement, Harvey's mother, Selena England, had identified the armed man who shot Isaiah, Susie, and her as Ben Krebs. Harvey told the court that he "did not recognize Krebs as one of the three men." Harvey did say that the man who had pointed a gun at him on the porch of the England home looked like Bill Taylor, brother of Rhoda Krebs and Aaron Taylor. Harvey, who had been face-to-face with the pistol-brandishing intruder on the porch that night, described the killer as a tall, thin, fair-complexioned man with a rag tied round his bare head, while his two accomplices wore rags tied around their beards.[45]

Attempting to further weaken the prosecution's argument by casting doubt on James Preston's and Aaron Taylor's involvement in the killings, defense lawyers called Mrs. E. T. Vanhooser, Mrs. Fannie Vanhooser, and S. J. Poland. All three were present at the Music home when Selena England made her dying declarations. Both Vanhooser women said that they had conversed with Selena as she lay mortally wounded, and Selena told them that "if James Preston was present at the time she was wounded and her husband killed, she did not know it." S. J. Poland stated that Selena had told those gathered by her bed that "the man she saw cutting her husband's throat was about the size of James Preston," but when asked if James Preston had participated in the crime, Selena replied, "no."[46]

Defense attorneys Grigsby and Willis pointed out that at no time during her various deathbed statements did Selena England implicate Aaron Taylor, who was a neighbor and well known to her. In addition, they objected to the inclusion of Selena's comments as to what her daughter Susie had said on August 26, namely, that, "old Ben Krebs is murdering us, he has come to kill us," because it was hearsay evidence. Judge Carroll overruled the defense objections.[47]

The remaining testimony and closing arguments by counsel took little time, and on the second day, November 11, 1876, Judge Carroll issued seven pages of detailed instructions to the jury before they started their deliberations. One of these, which greatly frustrated Krebs's attorneys, specifically directed, "The dying declarations of Selena England as detailed by the witnesses, having been admitted in the testimony, are to be considered by the jury in deliberating upon their verdict." Another of Carroll's directives concerned malice aforethought, a key requirement in a first-degree murder conviction. For Krebs to be guilty of first-degree murder, he must have planned or premeditated killing the Englands. Ben Krebs's multiple threats against the Englands were admissible in court and jurors could consider them because they helped prove malice in the mind of the defendant at the time of the crime. After Carroll finished reading his instructions, the jury retired to deliberate Krebs's guilt.[48]

The jurors required little time to reach their verdict. The *Galveston Daily News* reported, "Ben Kribbs [sic], the principal in the terrible murders of the England family in Montague County, has been tried and sentenced to death. The jury were out only five minutes." In the courtroom, jury foreman Cash McDonald stood and read the verdict aloud, "We the juror [sic] find the Defendant guilty and sess [sic] his punishment deth [sic]." Krebs and his attorneys then demanded that each member of the jury be polled by the judge and declare their verdict in open court.[49]

After the jurors complied, Judge Carroll approved the verdict and ordered "the defendant Ben Kribs [*sic*] to be hanged by the neck until he is dead." Krebs's attorneys, Grigsby and Willis, filed a motion for a new trial, which the judge promptly denied. The lawyers then appealed the verdict to the Texas Court of Appeals. Judge Carroll instructed that while the case was on appeal, Sheriff Perkins was to keep Krebs in the county jail and the prisoner was to pay all expenses incurred during his incarceration. In exchange for their legal fees, Ben and Rhoda Krebs transferred some of their acreage in the Wiley B. Savage Survey to the attorneys.[50]

In recognition of the unsettled conditions on the North Texas frontier, the State of Texas took extra security precautions during Krebs's trial to "prevent trouble and bloodshedding." Sheriff Perkins, given his slender resources, likely appreciated the backup. Maj. John B. Jones, commanding the Texas Frontier Battalion, ordered his subordinate, Lieutenant Campbell, and a company of men to Montague to guard Ben Krebs in custody. As a result, there were no attempts to lynch Krebs. The *Galveston Daily News* commended the frontier battalion for preventing any trouble at the jail "and causing many lawless men in our county to flee to more favorable regions to carry on their nefarious works. The people of this county owe a debt of gratitude to Major Jones and his command for their assistance."[51]

During the fall of 1876, incidents in Montague County aggravated tensions already elevated to a fevered pitch by the England homicides and Krebs's trial. The first was the killing of Montague County Deputy Sheriff Broaddus by a prisoner named George Wilson. The slaying of the sheriff's deputy "alarmed and excited" local residents. The second event was the murder trial of George Brown. George, brothers Andrew and Jesse, and their father, George Brown Sr., were all members of the Law and Order League, the notorious Montague County vigilante group that killed fourteen people during its heyday from 1872 to 1876.[52]

Major Jones's Frontier Battalion again provided security for Judge Carroll's Montague courtroom during the Brown trial. Authorities moved subsequent legal proceedings for George and Andrew Brown to Denton County because people in Montague County "were so wrought up." Following the Krebs and Brown trials in the fall of 1876, the *Galveston Daily News* trumpeted that Major Jones and his men had "thoroughly purged" Montague County "of its bad characters and law and order [had been] restored"—a statement that proved premature.[53]

—— 4 ——

It would be a year before the Texas Court of Appeals ruled on Ben Krebs's motion for a new trial. When the court finally considered his case on November 24, 1877, it agreed that his appeal had merit and sent the case back to North Texas for a second trial. In their opinion, the justices wrote that the Montague County jury had not specified whether the defendant was guilty of first-degree or second-degree murder, as required by law.[1]

In addition, the court found that District Judge Joseph Alexander Carroll had erred in putting Krebs on trial promptly, rather than granting him a continuance, as Carroll had done with both Preston and Taylor. After the England murders, the Montague County grand jury had jointly indicted all three of the accused. Texas statutes stipulated that when a court granted one or more jointly accused defendants a continuance, as with Preston and Taylor, all should receive a continuance, which would include Krebs. Presiding Court of Appeals Justice Matthew Duncan Ector wrote, "Our experience teaches us that often in the plainest cases the courts of the country, in their zeal to punish crime, deprive defendants of legal rights." Ector admonished the prosecutors and Judge Carroll that justice was served best by sticking to established procedures.[2]

The trials for the two remaining England murder suspects, Aaron Taylor and James Preston, got underway in the summer of 1877. In June, Montague County Attorney Avery Lenoir Matlock informed Judge Carroll that he was ready to proceed with Taylor's trial. Testimony started on June 11, 1877, and by the end of the following day, the jury had reached a verdict of guilty of murder in the first degree. Since Aaron Taylor was sixteen when the murders occurred, the maximum penalty the jury could assess under state law was life in prison. Taylor's attorneys, Grigsby and Willis, filed a motion for a new trial, which Judge Carroll denied.[3]

Grigsby and Willis next submitted an appeal to the Texas Court of Appeals. In September, Aaron Taylor settled his legal bill with the attorneys by assigning them his share of the William H. Taylor Survey. Two months later, on November 28, 1877, the appeals court considered Taylor's case and upheld the Montague County jury verdict. Justice Clinton McKamy Winkler, who wrote the opinion, stated that no errors had been found in the trial proceedings, and the verdict was confirmed.[4]

On June 13, 1878, Montague County Sheriff Lee Perkins brought Aaron Taylor back before Judge Carroll for a final hearing. The judge asked Taylor if he would like to make a statement, but the teenager "had naught to say." Carroll reaffirmed the jury's verdict, sentencing the youth to hard labor for the rest of his natural life at the state prison in Huntsville and ordering him to pay all of his trial and jail expenses. The sheriff then took the prisoner back to his cell. Five days later, on June 18, 1878, authorities transferred Aaron K. Taylor to the state prison in Huntsville to begin serving his life sentence.[5]

Next up for trial was James Preston. On June 11, 1877, the same day that Taylor's trial began, Preston appeared before Judge Carroll, where he pled not guilty to the murder indictment. When County Attorney Matlock announced that the county was ready to go to trial, defense attorneys Grigsby and Willis filed a change of venue motion. Noting Krebs's conviction, the defense argued that Preston could not receive a fair and impartial hearing from residents of Montague County.[6]

The defense attorneys collected affidavits from nine county residents supporting the change of venue. Preston requested that his trial be held in Henrietta, the county seat of Clay County, the next county to the west. Judge Carroll agreed to the change of venue, but instead of selecting Henrietta, he ordered the trial moved to Gainesville in neighboring Cooke County to the east. Preston then applied for bail, which Carroll denied.[7]

Preston's trial commenced on July 9, 1877, in Gainesville, and once again, Judge Carroll was the presiding judge. Defense attorneys quickly pinpointed a major flaw in the prosecution's case; namely, that Preston had no motive for participating in the England murders. In fact, he enjoyed a good relationship with the family and was personally in their debt. The Prestons and the Englands had been on friendly terms before the murders. When James Preston's wife, Martha, fell sick in early 1876, Selena England and Susie Taylor helped care for her. When Martha died a short time later, Rev. William England gave the sermon at her funeral.[8]

Ultimately, this line of defense failed to sway jurors, and the change of venue proved of no benefit to Preston. The Cooke County jury found Preston guilty of murder in the first degree and sentenced him to death. Grigsby and Willis immediately appealed this verdict to the Texas Court of Appeals. To settle his legal expenses, Preston and his children transferred to Grigsby and Willis title to acreage they jointly owned. When the Court of Appeals finally heard his case several months later on November 15, 1877, it found procedural errors in Preston's trial and overturned the jury's verdict. Presiding Justice Matthew Duncan Ector wrote the court's opinion.[9]

Preston's appeal pointed out that the defense had sent out multiple writs of attachment for trial witnesses to sheriffs in several North Texas counties. None of these writs was returned, with the result that witnesses crucial to Preston's case never showed up in court. Two of these witnesses, John and Luna Music, could have testified that Selena England never implicated Preston in the killings. While the mortally wounded Selena was lying in their home, she told the Musics that James Preston was not one of the murderers and that "Preston had always been friendly towards herself and family, and that there had never been any difficulty or hard feeling between them."[10]

In another important aspect of this testimony, when Harvey Taylor came to the Music home after the murders to visit his mother, Selena, John Music was out of the room. Luna was however present. Luna was prepared to testify that Harvey told Selena that he was reclining on the porch when the killers came up to the England house, and that the first man who approached him brandishing a pistol was Bill Taylor, brother of Aaron Taylor and Rhoda Krebs. Harvey also told his mother that one of the other murderers looked like John Music, Luna's husband.[11]

In his opinion on Preston's appeal, Court of Appeals Justice Ector wrote that Judge Carroll erred in allowing the jury in the Preston trial to hear testimony about the threats Ben Krebs made against the England family. Krebs's threats had nothing to do with Preston and may have influenced the jurors against him. In addition, Ector noted that although Selena England believed that Krebs was the first man on the porch and the one who had chased her and Susie, she was unsure of the identity of the second man she saw cutting her husband's throat.[12]

In his opinion, Ector made clear that overturning a murder conviction such as Preston's should not be commonplace. The justice recognized how important it was for the verdicts of local juries to be upheld and for the courts to adhere firmly to Texas laws. Ector wrote that it was paramount for citizens to understand they would be punished if they broke the law. This certainty of punishment was essential in safeguarding society. If authorities failed in their responsibilities to prosecute and convict lawbreakers, then those who had been injured or wronged would lose faith in the criminal justice system and resort to vigilantism.[13]

These points notwithstanding, Ector noted the law also required that before a person was executed, he must receive a just and unprejudiced trial and be legally convicted. If, upon appeal, it was shown that a defendant had been denied his rights, then the appeals court had no choice but to overturn his sentence and grant him a new trial. Without a fair appeals process, there would be no check against errors made by judges and juries. "God forbid that the prisoner should be sent to pray of the mercy of the executive [Governor of Texas] a reprieve for an offense of which he has not been legally convicted."[14]

The Texas Court of Appeals sent Preston's case back to Cooke County for a new trial. The prosecution tried James Preston for a second time in Gainesville in July 1878, once again in Judge Carroll's District Court. The jury found Preston guilty of first-degree murder and assessed the death penalty. Preston's defense attorneys again appealed. The Court of Appeals heard Preston's second appeal on February 11, 1880. Arguing for the State of Texas were Assistant Attorney General Thomas Ball and Thomas W. Dodd. Presenting the defense's case were William Grigsby, Frank Willis, James Mann Hurt, W. J. Sparks, Lucas F. Smith, and several other attorneys. Appeals Justice George W. Clark authored the court's opinion on Preston's second appeal.[15]

Clark had recently joined the appeals court in November 1879, replacing Presiding Justice Matthew Duncan Ector, who had died the preceding month. In assessing Clark's opinion, it is clear that he viewed the case very differently than his predecessor, Justice Ector, had. Beginning with Krebs's involvement, Clark felt that no impartial person could read the trial transcript and not conclude that Ben Krebs "was present at the assassination of the England family and a guilty participant . . . murdering with his own hands two helpless and inoffensive women." Clark noted that Susie Taylor, "when pursued and mortally wounded by the relentless assassin, . . . with her dying breath fixed the identity of Krebs." Clark concluded that although Selena England was unable to identify the other two attackers, she stated on several occasions and to multiple witnesses that she clearly recognized Krebs as the man chasing her and Susie.[16]

Selena's deathbed statements were spoken "with vivid recollection and exactness and convey to the mind at once a profound impression of the honesty and certainty of her convictions." Justice Clark opined that "murder will out" and that the "murdered women testify that Krebs was there, although their lips are sealed in death." Clark claimed that it was impossible for Selena to have mistaken Krebs, "His voice as it uttered its horrid curses, his beard, his hat, and her immediate proximity to him, so close that she could have put her hand upon him."[17]

Regarding Preston's involvement, Justice Clark concluded there was no doubt that Preston was with Krebs on the night of the murders as Preston had acknowledged spending the night with the Krebs family at their home. Since Preston admitted that he was with Ben Krebs all night, it followed that if Krebs was present at the England home when the murders took place, then Preston was there too. Clark attempted to downplay the most glaring weakness in the case against Preston; namely, that he had no motive to kill the Englands and in fact was on friendly terms with them. The justice agreed that the prosecution had not proven a motive for Preston's involvement but insisted that having a motive was not essential in securing a conviction.[18]

As a substitute for lack of motive, Justice Clark proffered his personal perspective on human nature and psychology: "Who with mortal ken can fathom the human heart and expose all its mysterious promptings? Crimes, the most horrible are often committed without apparent motive save an insatiate deviltry which mocks at social restraint and recklessly defies the laws of God and man." Clark suggested that Preston was influenced, seduced, or contaminated by Krebs's "evil and malicious heart" to participate in the murders.[19]

In summing up his court opinion, Clark noted that although it was possible Preston was innocent, he could not say that the jury had been mistaken in their verdict. "Appreciating to the fullest extent the grave consequences which must result from our action, and our responsibility to the law," Clark said, "we can reach no other conclusion that the appellant is guilty under the law and should suffer its penalty." With his appeals exhausted, James Preston now faced a date with the hangman.[20]

Like Preston, Ben Krebs was quickly running out of legal options. In February 1879, Krebs found himself before Judge Carroll once again, this time in a Gainesville courtroom. A Cooke County jury deliberated only twenty minutes before finding Krebs guilty and sentencing him to death. Reporting on the case, the *Galveston Daily News* added its own verdict: "Ben Kribbs [*sic*], who murdered the England family in Montague County, Texas, in 1876, has just been convicted of murder of the first degree in Cooke County District Court, where the case was taken on a change of venue, and will swing in a short time. . . . The criminal is described as a small, sunken-eyed shallow-pated and hardened-looking wretch." The *San Antonio Daily Express* offered its own glib commentary: "They are going to have a neck-tie social in Cooke County soon, but the main feature of the performance won't come off until Kribbs [*sic*] gets there. He will feel a little above the rest, but that's no odds, he'll soon come down."[21]

After this second conviction, Ben Krebs appealed his case a second time to the Texas Court of Appeals. Once again, he and Rhoda settled their legal expenses by transferring title to additional acreage to the Grigsby & Willis law firm. This time, the transfer included their homestead and surrounding property. On February 11, 1880, the Court of Appeals convened to hear arguments from both the prosecution and defense attorneys. Assistant Attorney General Thomas Ball spoke for the state, while W. J. Sparks, Grigsby and Willis, and N. P. Jackson represented Krebs. Justice John Preston White wrote the court's opinion. In explaining the justices' decision, White failed to address a key element of Harvey Taylor's testimony; namely, that Harvey was certain neither Krebs nor Aaron Taylor were the murderers.[22]

Justice White did discuss but was dismissive of Harvey's statement that one of the killers looked like Bill Taylor and that a second man resembled John Music. White also discounted assertions by John Walker, Joseph Cothrum, and Wilborn Cothrum, who were unable testify at Krebs's second trial due to scheduling conflicts. All three men were prepared to testify that they saw and conversed with Bill Taylor and two associates on the morning after the murders. Krebs's defense attorneys had requested a continuance so that the three men might have time to travel to Gainesville and testify, but District Judge Carroll had denied the motion. Justice White wrote "as to the other three witnesses, John Walker, Joseph and Wilborn Cothrum, if they had been present, they would not have been permitted to testify to Bill Taylor's statements and declarations, because such testimony would have been hearsay and inadmissible."[23]

Here are three eyewitnesses who met Bill Taylor and two other men the day after the England murders. Walker's and the Cothrums' combined statements presented compelling evidence that the state may have convicted the wrong men, but White was not interested in other possible suspects. Ironically, White rejected Walker's and the Cothrums' evidence out of hand as hearsay while accepting hearsay testimony from witnesses who had paraphrased Selena England's deathbed statements.[24]

This contradiction raises an important point regarding hearsay testimony. The hearsay rule in general did not allow statements made outside of court to be introduced as evidence in a trial. Texas legal historian Michael Ariens notes, however, that the hearsay rule "was riddled with many exceptions, so a number of out-of-court statements were admitted as evidence. The justifications for admitting hearsay evidence were either reliability or necessity."[25]

One exception to the hearsay rule was the dying declaration. Dying declarations such as Selena England's were admissible in court, providing that they adhered to established legal criteria. For example, if a person knew their death was at hand, made a statement regarding the circumstances of their death, and later died, a witness to that dying declaration could testify as to what they heard. Such statements were only admissible in murder trials. Michael Ariens says that in reality the application of this criterion was uneven. In some cases, "it appears that dying declarations were admitted as evidence because greater stress was placed on the necessity of their admission, rather than their reliability."[26]

The admissibility of dying declarations has its roots in a 1789 case, *The King v. Woodcock*. It was assumed that someone on their deathbed, who had no hope of life and believed death was imminent, would not lie knowing they were about to meet their maker. In a dying person, "every motive to falsehood is silenced, . . . the mind is induced by the most powerful considerations to speak the truth." Persons making dying declarations would be afraid of "heaven's ultimate punishment for false testimony—[for violating] . . . one of the Ten Commandments."[27]

Of course, this hearsay exception assumes that a person making a dying declaration would not maliciously lie, because they believe in God, hell, and an afterlife. But what about someone who is not religious? Or someone who is amoral and has no conscience? Knowing they were going to die and could not be charged with perjury, they could seek revenge upon others by making false statements. In fact, many courts made "no attempt to ascertain the belief system of the declarant. Without the belief in eternal damnation, the main guarantor of trustworthiness is gone."[28]

In Selena England's case, her dying declarations were likely viewed as unimpeachable. After all, she and her family were the victims of a terrible crime and there was considerable sympathy for her. In addition, people assumed that as the wife of a minister, she must be a devout person. But what if she had made a mistaken identification? Or what if in fact she was a vindictive woman who deliberately lied in order to get revenge on Ben Krebs for their July 1876 fence-line confrontation? Authorities never delved into her background, religious convictions, or belief system.

Appeals Court Justice White obviously had no doubts about Selena's dying declarations, confidently stating that the jury could have reached no other verdict but guilty and that the appropriate punishment for anyone guilty of such a crime was death. White could "not see that any dispassionate mind could for a single moment hesitate, much less doubt" Krebs's guilt. "He is positively identified by those dying exclamations of Susie Taylor, 'Oh mother! Old Ben Krebs has come to kill us all,' and 'Oh mother, Ben Krebs has killed me;' and again by Mrs. England, who, conscious of her approaching death, told him, when brought into her presence for identification, 'that she was not mistaken; that he was the man who did it.'"[29]

White pointed out that Selena recognized Krebs "by his whiskers, by his Dutch talk [Swiss accent] and curses, and she said she even knew him by the old white hat he was then holding in his hands." In a condescending nod to Krebs's attorneys, White noted that, "while able counsel for the accused, with untiring energy, have exerted all their skill and ability, . . . the State has fully made out and established his guilt. We find in the record of his conviction no error entitling him to another trial, and the judgment against him is therefore in all things affirmed."[30]

After the Court of Appeals upheld their convictions, Ben Krebs and James Preston were taken before Judge Carroll for final sentencing. Carroll turned to Preston and asked him if he had anything to say on his behalf to show why he should not receive the death penalty. Preston rose from his chair and addressed the judge: "I am fully sensible that I can say nothing now that would be effective, but I cannot permit the opportunity to pass without saying that I know I am innocent, and that though my life be forfeited, I thank God that this conscious knowledge of innocence cannot be destroyed." Preston then sat down.[31]

Carroll then asked Ben Krebs the same question he had posed to Preston. A heavily shackled Krebs rose from his chair. His voice trembling with emotion, Ben acknowledged that he had been legally convicted. There was much that he wanted to say, but he felt his poor command of the English language might cause his remarks to be misunderstood. In addition, whatever he might have to say would not change his sentence. Krebs concluded his remarks with a strong statement of innocence. "I see a large company here present," he said, "and I want to say to the court, in the hearing of the country, that I am not the murderer of the England family, and the perpetrators of that crime are not here." After Preston and Krebs finished addressing the court, Judge Carroll set the time and place of their hanging for April 30, 1880, at Gainesville, Texas.[32]

At this point, Krebs and Preston had each been tried and convicted by two separate juries. The Texas Court of Appeals had reviewed their cases twice. During this period, the appeals court reversed on average 65 percent of all convictions. These reversals were largely based on three types of errors: indictments, trial evidence, and jury instructions. In their first round of appeals, Krebs and Preston secured conviction reversals largely because of legal errors. By the time of their second appeals, however, all critical mistakes and technicalities had, in the minds of the justices, been resolved.[1]

Generally, in the Anglo-American criminal justice system, authority is divided between judge and jury. The judge rules on any legal issues that arise during a trial, while the jury, in its verdict, decides questions of fact. Despite evidence that could have given pause to some, the Texas Court of Appeals refused to seriously consider other credible scenarios or suspects in the England family murders. Michael Ariens, an expert on Texas's nineteenth-century legal system, points out that, "One institutional aspect that you have to be careful of [at that time], appellate judges in particular are loath to disturb the factual findings of a jury, even if they have harbored doubts, unless there is something that shows that this is against the great weight of the evidence. Even if they say they have doubts they will not overturn a verdict."[2]

On April 22, 1880, two months after the Court of Appeals upheld Krebs's and Preston's convictions, the *Denison Daily News* reported that the pair was to be hung, along with a third man named L. M. Noftsinger, at Gainesville on April 30. A jury had convicted Noftsinger for murdering his rival in a classic love triangle. Noftsinger's girlfriend had left him for another man, whom she subsequently married. The jilted Noftsinger then sneaked into the couple's house while they were sleeping and shot the husband in the head. The *Daily News* noted that the Gainesville gallows for the triple hanging had been conveniently constructed near the railroad tracks. "It will be a free exhibition, and it is expected that thousands of people will be present. To accommodate those wishing to go from Denison," the railroad "will probably put on a special train and give reduced rates of fare."[3]

On April 22, W. J. Walters, a reporter for the *Galveston Daily News*, paid a visit to Krebs and Preston at the Gainesville jail. Walters wrote, "The unfortunate men seem resigned to their fate. Preston still hopes for executive clemency. Krebs is bitter against the press, as he says they have not dealt fairly with him but have educated people to the belief that he is guilty." Walters estimated that up to ten thousand people might watch Krebs, Preston, and Noftsinger hang.[4]

On April 24, 1880, Texas Governor Oran Milo Roberts upended the England murder case by commuting Krebs's and Preston's death sentences to life sentences at hard labor in the state penitentiary. In all criminal cases excluding treason or impeachment, the Texas Constitution gave the governor the power to grant commutations and pardons. Roberts, who was himself an attorney and former chief justice of the Texas Supreme Court, had made a careful and deliberate study of the England family murders. Before publicly announcing the commutations, however, Roberts sent a private note to the firm of Cunningham and Ellis, which was operating the Huntsville Prison under lease from the State of Texas. Roberts advised the business partners that he had signed commutations for Krebs and Preston. The governor instructed Cunningham and Ellis to go to Gainesville and transport the prisoners to Huntsville before April 30, the date previously set for their execution.[5]

On April 26, two days after commuting Krebs's and Preston's sentences, Roberts declined to exercise executive clemency on behalf of L. M. Noftsinger. After reviewing the evidence, the governor was satisfied of Noftsinger's guilt. Roberts fully expected that Krebs's and Preston's commutations would ignite a firestorm, especially in the North Texas region where the England murders occurred. Worried that the commutations and Noftsinger's execution on April 30 might spark vigilante reprisals, including lynching Krebs and Preston in the Gainesville jail, the governor wanted the pair out of town well in advance.[6]

Ironically, the primary impetus for Roberts's intervention in the Krebs and Preston cases came from District Judge Joseph Alexander Carroll, the judge who had presided over all five trials of Ben Krebs, James Preston, and Aaron Taylor in Montague and Cooke Counties. Judge Carroll worried that a terrible, irreversible wrong was about to occur if authorities executed Krebs and Preston. On April 5, 1880, the judge penned a letter to Governor Roberts, asking him to commute their sentences to life in prison. Carroll wrote that if he were persuaded beyond a reasonable doubt that Krebs and Preston were guilty, he would support their death sentences. The judge noted that the England case had been before him numerous times during the last four years. He had studied the evidence and the testimony of various witnesses with great interest. Carroll felt it his duty to convey his reservations to the governor before it was too late.[7]

Describing the England family murders as "a shocking crime, perhaps unequaled in the annals of crime in Texas," Roberts wrote in his commutations that both he and Judge Carroll had a "lingering substantial apprehension" about Krebs's and Preston's guilt. Their reservations were shared by many lawyers, prominent people, and average citizens who had written to the governor, asking him to intervene in the case. In explaining his commutations, Roberts noted that he had carefully reviewed all the details in the England case twice.[8]

One important unanswered question regarding Carroll's letter is why the judge waited so long to act. Why did he not intercede earlier, when he was overseeing the five murder trials over a four-year period? It appears that Carroll waited until the last possible minute, when his conscience told him that Krebs and Preston would die unless he helped them. Texas legal historian Michael Ariens explains, "The presiding judge is permitted to say in a criminal case, 'You, the prosecution, have not shown sufficient evidence as a matter of law that the jury could find this person guilty. I am simply acquitting the defendant as a matter of law.'" But as Ariens points out, "this is very unusual because of the double jeopardy provision. Once the judge does that you can't try the defendant again. And remember that the judge is an elected figure. If the judge does that contrary to the members of the community, he's not going to get re-elected." Indeed, the intense backlash that Carroll experienced after he wrote Governor Roberts may well have been the motivating factor in his January 1881 decision not to seek re-election.[9]

On the morning of April 29, 1880, Cunningham and Ellis, managers of the state prison, took custody of Krebs and Preston at the Gainesville jail and boarded the eleven o'clock train to Huntsville. Governor Roberts's premonition proved correct. The *Galveston Daily News* reported that a large mob from Montague County descended upon the Gainesville depot shortly after the train pulled out, intent on lynching Krebs and Preston. The newspaper article noted that in Montague County, "where the atrocious murder was committed," residents were furious. Citizens were indignant over the commutations, and much of their hostility was focused on Judge Carroll and his letter, which Governor Roberts had quoted in the commutations. In an interview with the *Daily News*, Krebs and Preston both emphatically declared their innocence. Preston was grateful for the governor's commutation, but Krebs said that Roberts had not done him any favors. Krebs preferred hanging to spending the rest of his life in prison at hard labor.[10]

Another report from Gainesville appearing in the same issue of the *Galveston Daily News* mentioned that feelings were running high against Roberts and Carroll, who were to be burned in effigy. Although the third man scheduled to hang on April 30, L. M. Noftsinger, had freely admitted his guilt, it was rumored that some two hundred people would make an attempt to rescue him. Apparently, the crowd congregating in Gainesville for his hanging felt that if "villains" such as Krebs and Preston could escape the death penalty, then executive clemency "should be made universal."[11]

The Cooke County sheriff was forced to move the scaffold for Noftsinger's execution more than a mile out of town after the landowners refused to allow the hanging on their property. An erroneous rumor circulating in Gainesville claimed that the move was necessitated after a mob knocked down and destroyed the platform. In any case, Sheriff Ozment expressed full confidence that any attempt to rescue Noftsinger would be swiftly suppressed. The sheriff had sworn in extra deputies, and the city marshal had also implemented extra precautions. Media reports mentioned that large crowds from Montague, Clay, Wise, Denton, and Cooke Counties were flooding into town. By the next day, more than ten thousand people, the largest gathering in Gainesville's history, had assembled around the scaffold to view the city's third legal hanging.[12]

Noftsinger's execution was scheduled for the afternoon of April 30, 1880, and several newspapers from around the state were on hand to cover the event. The *Denison Daily News* reporter mixed among the crowd, where an intense anger prevailed. Many of those present expressed overt sympathy for Noftsinger, believing that a great wrong was about to be committed and that he was "far more worthy of clemency than the murderers of the English [sic] family." A number of onlookers proposed demonstrating their contempt for the governor by stopping

Noftsinger's execution. The Denison paper observed that if the gathered throng had found "a bold, determined leader, there might have been trouble."[13]

Shortly after four o'clock, Noftsinger climbed the scaffold and the sheriff adjusted the noose around his neck. Suddenly, Zack Calloway, a noted outlaw, jumped forward and tried to cut the rope. The sheriffs of Hunt and Collin Counties, who were assisting with crowd control, blocked the attempt and took Calloway into custody. At this point, the crowd became more restive, with some shouting, "He shan't be hung, cut the rope," and others crying, "turn him loose, let's not see him murdered, boys." Some of the spectators then rushed the gallows but were prevented from reaching Noftsinger by Sheriff Ozment and his deputies, who with pistols drawn, blocked access to the platform.[14]

Then, some in the back of the crowd panicked, causing a stampede, "during which men, women and children were forced to the ground and swept over by those before them, amid wagons and horses plunging wildly to the rear." A clergyman, Reverend Hening, implored everyone to calm down, and after a short time, the bedlam ceased. Just before 4:30 P.M., the gallows' trap door opened and Noftsinger was "launched in eternity." Newspaper reports lauded the brave, steadfast law enforcement officials who with their "courage and coolness averted what might have become a dreadful affray in which many lives would have been sacrificed."[15]

Following Noftsinger's execution, the controversy surrounding Governor Roberts's commutations continued unabated. Some public commentary was positive, but much was scathingly negative. In one approving editorial, the *Dallas Daily Herald* reminded readers that Texas's chief executive was "a man of irreproachable integrity and sterling force of character, . . . a legal light learned in the law, skilled in criminal procedure," through his years as a district attorney and district judge. Prior to his election as governor in 1878, Roberts served on the Texas Supreme Court for more than ten years, including five years as its chief justice. In the Dallas paper's view, "The presumption therefore is not only fair but logical that of all men Governor Roberts is pre-eminently qualified to pass upon the value of any exercise of executive clemency in behalf of criminals condemned to the gallows." The fact that Roberts ordered these widely unpopular commutations while running for re-election reflects his integrity and also suggests how strongly he believed in his course of action.[16]

In marked contrast, the *Fort Griffin Echo* was blistering in its denunciation of both Governor Roberts and Judge Carroll. The newspaper described the England case as "one of the most brutal and atrocious murders ever heard in the annals of crime." The *Echo* was at a loss to understand how the governor could in good conscience commute Krebs's and Preston's sentences, and why, if Judge Carroll had such reservations concerning their guilt, he had not ordered new trials for them. The editors opined that the governor's actions were "nothing less than an inducement for crime and an open rebuke to juries and courts from doing their duties."[17]

The *Galveston Daily News* noted that some North Texas residents had sent Governor Roberts postcards threatening "some direful punishment." In the *Dallas Daily Herald*, a reporter from Montague County cursed Roberts "unmercifully," and reported that locals in Montague and Cooke Counties believed bribes had been paid to secure the commutations for "these bloody villains." The last rumor is ludicrous when one considers that the Krebs and Preston families, both of very limited means before the England murders, had sold their property and exhausted their meager funds to pay jail expenses and attorney's fees for all of the trials and appeals.[18]

A writer for the *Denison Daily News* wrote that the public firestorm sparked by Roberts's actions was more than justified. Over a four-year period, five separate juries composed of a total of sixty men had all found the defendants guilty. What more was needed? The reporter, who had attended Preston's trial in 1878, could not understand anyone doubting that "these two villains" had committed the crime. He called the England case "the most beastly that ever disgraced the country in all the annals of crime. None can be found more cruel and heinous, and if mortal man ever deserved the gallows these two certainly." To the reporter, Judge Carroll's letter to the governor was incomprehensible. He recalled that during Preston's trial, the judge's instructions to the jury had been far from impartial. No one present in the courtroom could have doubted that Carroll favored conviction. A *Fort Worth Democrat* editorial said that the public should never trust an indecisive judge like Carroll who affirmed the jury's verdict while believing the defendant innocent.[19]

The *Denison Daily News* reported that a petition to pardon Krebs and Preston was circulating throughout Texas. Local opinion regarding both men was still hostile, however. The newspaper predicted that if the governor were to pardon them and they attempted to return to Montague County, they would be lynched. In fact, members of both families did eventually move from North Texas to Indian Territory (Oklahoma) after the commutations. Area residents continued to harbor bitter feelings against the two men for years.[20]

Rumors of pardons proved to be short-lived. Governor Roberts was not going to undermine his 1880 re-election campaign by further actions on behalf of Preston and Krebs. The commutations had already caused enough collateral damage. The governor's close friend Thomas H. Murray informed him that Finis E. Piner, the state district attorney who helped prosecute Krebs and Preston, had issued a rancorous denunciation of the governor. Piner was very upset with Roberts and he intended to write the full story of the England murders and upon completion, forward it to the *Galveston Daily News* for publication.[21]

One reason for Piner's anger was that the governor had failed to consult him before issuing the commutations. Piner told Murray that the governor had lost Denton, Montague, and Cooke Counties in his re-election through his actions, and that he was going to go in person to the state convention to oppose Roberts's nomination to a second term. Murray apprised the governor he had strongly advised Piner against this course of action and hoped that this counsel had calmed him down a bit. Nevertheless, Murray worried, "Piner might pack a convention against you and *this must be watched.*" After de-escalating Piner, Murray strolled around Denton, Texas, and polled a number of people regarding their feelings on the commutations. One of his stops was at the district clerk's office.[22]

At the clerk's office, Denton County Judge Thomas Elisha Hogg, younger brother of future Texas Governor James Stephen Hogg, mentioned to Murray that several trustworthy people at Whitesboro in Grayson County had told him "no person ought ever to be convicted even on the dying statement of the England family." Hogg believed them. Murray said that Hogg's statement sparked a lively discussion among those assembled regarding Selena England's character. "An old farmer in the party said he had lived by the England family [for] five years; that they were the meanest and most-quarrelsome set he ever knew; that Ms. [Selena] England brought up her boys to learn and do, therefore, whatever was outrageous and mean, and that he would believe nothing any of them would say." His polling concluded, Thomas Murray closed his remarks to Roberts on a positive note, stating that most residents still supported the governor.[23]

Roberts's actions created stiff political headwinds, but nothing strong enough to prevent him from securing the Democratic Party's nomination for re-election. Writing to the governor from Montague County, Krebs's and Preston's attorneys, William H. Grigsby and Frank Willis, extended their felicitations: "Sir; Allow us to congratulate you for we are truly glad you succeeded in getting the nomination. . . . A few designing shysters here worked upon the prejudices of the people at our delegate convention and succeeded in getting an opposition delegation because of the Preston-Krebs commutation. We assure you that those of our citizens who are best informed in regard to your action in that matter fully endorse your reasons for interfering in their behalf." Grigsby and Willis closed their remarks by stating how pleased they were to have Roberts atop the Democratic ticket once again and promised the governor strong support from North Texas in the upcoming election.[24]

Although Roberts's actions on behalf of Krebs and Preston generated considerable controversy at the time, if one examines the governor's record on commutations and pardons during his tenure, it is clear he followed an established pattern of executive clemency typical for the period. While he was governor, Roberts commuted ten murder in the first degree death sentences, including those of Krebs and Preston, to life in prison. He also pardoned ten life sentences for murder. Never once did he take the full step of pardoning someone convicted of murder in the first degree who had been sentenced to death. There was always a two-step process: death to life in prison, and life in prison to pardon. Many of those serving life sentences for murder were not pardoned by Roberts until they had served ten to twenty years and had clearly demonstrated good behavior and a record of rehabilitation.[25]

Reflecting upon the considerable public indignation over Krebs's and Preston's commutations, a *Galveston Daily News* writer felt that perhaps at least part of the blame lay with the deficiencies of Texas's inequitable legal system. The reporter observed that some of the anger directed at the governor might better be focused upon the state's pliable court of appeals and upon juries that failed to condemn killers, most notably killers who were wealthy and had influential friends. Ben Krebs and James Preston, their death sentences now commuted to life at hard labor, had neither wealth nor influential friends.[26]

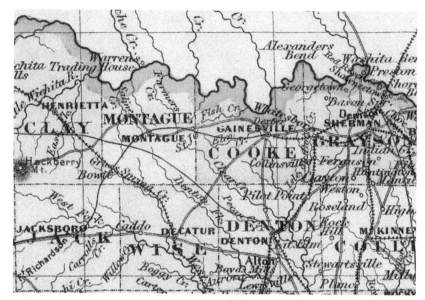

Detail of North Texas from *A. J. Johnson's 1886 Map of Texas. Courtesy of the David Rumsey Historical Map Collection.*

Old rock-lined well and artifacts from the England homestead in the Thomas N. Savage Survey. *Photo by the author.*

Site of the Krebs homestead in the Wiley B. Savage Survey. *Photo by the author.*

Ben Krebs and Rhoda Krebs (*seated*) and family. *Courtesy of William Preston Krebs.*

Avery Lenoir Matlock, the Montague County attorney who prosecuted the England murder trials. *Courtesy of Texas State Preservation Board.*

Joseph Alexander Carroll, the Sixteenth Judicial District judge who presided over the England murder trials. Originally published in *History and Reminiscences of Denton County*, by Edward Franklin Bates, 1918.

One of the four England family graves at Ben Dye Cemetery near Whitesboro, Texas. *Photo by the author.*

Huntsville Prison in the 1870s. *Courtesy of Special Collections Library, Sam Houston State University.*

Huntsville Prison in the 1870s, southwest view. *Courtesy of Special Collections Library, Sam Houston State University.*

"Peckerwood Hill" cemetery at Huntsville Prison, circa 1899. Aaron Kendrick Taylor was buried here in June 1880. *Courtesy of Special Collections Library, Sam Houston State University.*

Rusk Penitentiary at Rusk, Texas. *Courtesy of Texas Prison Museum.*

Rear view of prison cells at Rusk Penitentiary. *Courtesy of Texas State Library and Archives Commission.*

Four of the five Texas governors involved in the England murder case. Seated (*left to right*): Oran Milo Roberts and James Stephen Hogg. Standing (*left to right*): Francis Richard Lubbock and Lawrence Sullivan "Sul" Ross. *Courtesy of Texas State Library and Archives Commission.*

Bonam Franklin Dickerson, holding grandson, and wife, Luna Broderick Smith Dickerson, former wife of John R. Music. *Courtesy of L. Hodges.*

Grave of William Barnett "Bill" Taylor, Fairview Cemetery, Vinita, Oklahoma. *Photo by the author.*

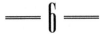

The first of those convicted in the England murders to begin serving his life sentence was Aaron Kendrick Taylor. The eighteen-year-old Taylor, Convict No. 6870, entered Huntsville State Penitentiary on June 18, 1878. Upon arrival, he and the other new prisoners received a shave and a close haircut. Prison guards made a detailed description of every incoming inmate, recording any birthmarks, tattoos, or other prominent features that could help in identifying the convict should he escape. Taylor's convict register listed him as 5 feet, 8 inches tall, 140 pounds, with blue eyes, light hair, and scars on his lower back and on the front of his neck. An entry on Taylor's conduct certificate for December 21 of that year noted that prison officials ordered him confined to his cell for a day with only bread and water. They also suspended his letter-writing privileges. Apparently, he left his cell to play cards, both transgressions of prison regulations.[1]

Ben Krebs and James Preston arrived at Huntsville almost two years later, on May 1, 1880. Krebs, Convict No. 8619, was 52 years old, 5 feet, 9 inches tall, 156 pounds, with blue eyes and a bald head rimmed with brown hair. Shortly after his arrival, Krebs wrote to Rev. F. A. Heuring in Gainesville about prison life. Six days a week, inmates worked at their prison jobs, but on Sundays they were allowed to rest in their cells. On Sundays they were also permitted to receive and write letters. Krebs told the reverend that he had recently joined the Christian Association. Krebs said, "I am living in hopes that the truth may yet prevail, and that justice will be done . . . but if such should not be the will of God, then I shall look forward to a meeting in a happier world."[2]

Preston, Convict No. 8620, was 56 years old, 5 feet, 11 inches, and 170 pounds, with blue eyes and brown hair. He had a scar on the left side of his chest and his left hand was missing the third finger. Prison records indicate that officers punished Preston in September 1880, but do not detail the offense. Following Preston's incarceration at Huntsville, the Montague County Probate Court assigned a guardian for the five of his children who were still minors. The guardian, William J. Shields, paid for the support and care of John Warren, Mary, Olive, Georgia, and Elizabeth Preston by selling acreage that Preston owned.[3]

Krebs, Preston, and Taylor entered the Texas prison system during one of the darkest periods in its history. When they came to Huntsville an outside contractor was running the penitentiary under a lease from the State of Texas. While the state retained oversight of the prison, the lessees oversaw day-to-day operations. Texas prison historian Donald Walker says that the state, "in adopting the lease system, . . . abdicated virtually all responsibility for the welfare of its prisoners. As a result, the typical leased institution lodged prisoners who were poorly fed, poorly clothed, poorly housed, without proper medical care, and worked beyond reasonable limits."[4]

From 1871 to 1883, Texas leased out its prisons at Huntsville and Rusk to several businesses. The lessees were more concerned about making a profit than providing proper care for the inmates. State supervision was slipshod. In 1873–77, A. J. Ward, E. C. Dewey, and N. Patton, collectively known as Ward, Dewey, and Company, managed the prison system. In 1877, the state awarded the lease to a new firm, Edward H. Cunningham and Littleberry A. Ellis, who oversaw operations until 1883, when the state resumed control.[5]

In 1878, Texas had 1,738 prisoners. By 1894, the number had ballooned to 4,125. The inmate population always exceeded prison capacity. As a result, authorities housed convicts with lesser sentences in outside work camps. Railroads, lumber companies, sawmills, ironworks, and plantations leased prisoners to work at various locations in the eastern half of the state. Because escapes from these camps were frequent, the state confined inmates with life sentences, such as Krebs, Preston, and Taylor, within the walls of the penitentiary, which typically housed six hundred to eight hundred convicts. Even after the State of Texas resumed operation of its prisons in May 1883, it continued to lease out convict labor until 1912. The labor leases brought in badly needed revenue and helped reduce prison overcrowding, thus postponing the need to build expensive additional facilities.[6]

Conditions at the outside work camps were appalling. State prison inspector J. K. P. Campbell visited one site near present-day Lake Jackson, Texas, and discovered inmates who had not had a change of clothes for ten weeks. One-third of the convicts were sick, and none had received medical attention. For the meat portion of their diet convicts were served "hog chidings with the excrement still on them, and only half cooked." Guards were frequently vicious in dispensing punishment. Campbell noted, "I found convicts whose backs were cut to pieces in the most shocking manner."[7]

Fifty percent of the leased inmates worked on cotton and sugar plantations, including Edward Cunningham's and Littleberry Ellis's plantations in Fort Bend County near Houston. "When the state leased convicts out to private contractors [like Cunningham and Ellis], they had no financial interest in the health or welfare of the people working for them," notes Rice University professor W. Caleb McDaniel, "and so the convict-leasing system saw extremely high levels of mortality and sickness under convict lessees. If the prisoner died, they would simply go back to the state and say, 'You owe us another prisoner.'" Through their lease of the Texas prison system and its convicts, Cunningham & Ellis reportedly made more than $500,000 profit, while the State of Texas cleared almost $360,000.[8]

Throughout the prison-leasing era, inmates housed inside the prisons also experienced brutal and inhumane treatment. Donald Walker's research discovered, "The deplorable conditions that prevailed in the Texas prisons during the lease [period] . . . proved to be immune to any substantive attempts at remediation." Walker says, "Indeed, mistreatment of prisoners and the ruthless exploitation of their labor constituted veritable hallmarks of the system at the time." Typically, the inmates' daily diet featured a breakfast of bread (often cornbread), molasses, beef or bacon, and black coffee. Lunch consisted of beef or bacon soup, cornbread, and vegetables (when available). In the absence of vegetables, the men received navy beans, rice, hominy, or dried apples. Dinner featured cornbread with either beef or bacon. An 1876 report on the state penitentiary found that "the quality and variety of the food furnished the convicts . . . in many instances, . . . has been of a character to nauseate instead of satisfying the pangs of hunger."[9]

Edward Anson Hart arrived at Huntsville in the early 1880s, convicted of second-degree murder. Hart recalled that the prison diet consisted of cornbread, rancid bacon, and navy beans. Many inmates became ill and some came down with scurvy. Ailing convicts quickly learned that prison medical care could be injurious to their health. Hart tells of two cellmates, one young and the other middle-aged, who got sick one evening and were admitted to the prison hospital.

The hospital attendant, an inmate, gave them some medication and they both subsequently died. The next morning, the regular staff doctor examined the two men and discovered they had received the wrong medicine. When state investigators toured the hospital, they found it over capacity and excessively hot. Required medicines were missing or in short supply. The investigators' report noted, "We can find no excuse for such a departure from humanity, there is none."[10]

Sadistic and violent abuse of inmates by prison guards was a pernicious problem during the 1870s and 1880s, one that prison superintendents proved unable to stop. Donald Walker notes, "Even trivial offenses . . . could result in a punitive ordeal so severe that a gag had to be placed in the suffering prisoner's mouth to stifle the screams." Walker continues, "Guards often inflicted punishment at night so there would be no witnesses." Edward Anson Hart recalled two captains, one named Kelly and the other, Marion Ezell, who were well known for their harsh treatment of inmates.[11]

One new prisoner at the state penitentiary at Rusk, J. L. Wilkinson, quickly ran into problems with Captain Ezell. Wilkinson said of Ezell, "Every word, action and visage stamped him a cruel brute in everything but form, and thus I judged him." Wilkinson despised Ezell, saying, "How he ever got to be part of the system is beyond my power to explain . . . many of his underlings, getting their cues from him, never hesitated to be as brutal as he." The new convict claimed that the cruel captain "had killed twenty-six inmates by either beating them to death or working them until they dropped dead from sickness and exhaustion." Wilkinson says that Ezell relished disciplining prisoners and often exceeded the thirty-nine-lash maximum punishment, applying seventy-five to one hundred lashes.[12]

Wilkinson related the story of a teenaged prisoner with a delicate constitution who was too weak to work in the fields and had been hospitalized. Despite the prison doctor's recommendations that the youth remain in bed, Ezell ordered him back to work. While laboring outdoors, the teen came down with a fever and was returned to the prison hospital. Once again Ezell sent him back to the fields, where the youth got the chills, went into convulsions, and died. According to Wilkinson, Ezell claimed the teenager died from eating too many raw potatoes.[13]

Both Wilkinson and another convict named Henry Tomlin, who later wrote about his own prison experiences, offered additional examples of Marion Ezell's brutal behavior. In one instance, Ezell allegedly ordered a hospitalized prisoner named Moseley to accompany a detail of men to cut wood near the prison. Moseley, who had been in the hospital for several months, was "emaciated and sickly" and pled with Ezell that he was still unwell, but Ezell told him, "Go, or I will kick your guts out." On the second day out on this work crew, Moseley fell over and died while pulling on a crosscut saw. His body was left on the saw all day until the work crew loaded him on their wagon upon returning to the prison. Ezell reportedly expressed disbelief at Moseley's death, claiming that he was one of the more robust inmates at Rusk. According to Wilkinson, authorities recorded his death as occurring from natural causes.[14]

In his prison memoir, Henry Tomlin, who was convicted of rape and incarcerated at Rusk from 1889 to 1904, asserted that Ezell systematically tortured him for years and cited numerous instances of physical abuse. Tomlin stated that over time Marion Ezell's chronic sadism, manifested in both mental and physical abuse, reduced him to a partially paralyzed cripple. Tomlin did have an axe to grind when he penned his reminiscences. He was a recalcitrant and uncompliant inmate who often refused to work and went out of his way to undercut Ezell with his superiors. In his self-published account, Tomlin recalls Ezell grabbing a wooden bed slat and repeatedly beating a young inmate with mental illness before the youth managed to slip out of his cell and run into the courtyard dressed only in a shirt, frantically shouting for assistance. Ironically, Ezell, despised and feared by inmates, owed his life to an African American convict named Felix Jones. Jones rescued Ezell "when he was murderously assaulted" during an attempted prison escape.[15]

Describing other instances of prisoner mistreatment at Rusk, Edward Anson Hart recorded that an inmate named Mancho, who attempted to escape, was "stripped, laid on a cold rock floor, and hit, according to my count 150 lashes with the regulation strap, while the limit according to law is 39 strokes." Sadistic prison guards disproportionately targeted African American convicts for punishment. One black inmate received 150 lashes for trying to escape and another 39 lashes for a separate misdemeanor. "But not being satisfied with the work of the strap, Captain [F. P.] O'Brien took a bed slat and finished the job of beating that negro . . . they whipped the negro a double dose," Hart says, and "whenever they could find no excuse to whip anyone else they whipped that negro."[16]

Guards received $20 a month in salary. In comparison, the average monthly wage for a laborer or cowboy was $30. Many guards "had no qualifications for the job . . . and sought the position only as a last resort." State prison regulations stated that employees were "prohibited from using profane, indecent, or insulting language towards a convict" and were "at all times to be kind, dignified, and firm in their treatment" of inmates. In practice, guards fell far short of this stated ideal. Edward Anson Hart remembered, "The language used by nearly all the officials and by their assistants and sub-bosses is profane, coarse, and vulgar. Many of the guards and especially the prison tenders or turnkeys, are the very lowest and seem to gloat over the lowest, meanest and most debasing things." Guards would occasionally "insult the poor convicts' wives, daughters, or sisters" when they came to visit inmates.[17]

Penitentiary employees also turned a blind eye to the raping of inmates. Few of the new arrivals withstood such assaults. Hart recalled, "Sodomy is one of the worst evils of prison life and the hardened criminal with fiendish delight is often let into the cell of a young and fresh convict that he may prostitute his victim to hellish passion." Hart said that, "Many of the older convicts, when a young man is brought in, gloat over the fact, and they say to their elbow neighbor, 'that's my piece.'"[18]

A state investigation found that the lessees running the prison system were "drinking men, in many cases drinking to the extent of drunkenness," and that they were often inebriated inside the prison, in the presence of inmates. To make matters worse, "two of the lessees, Messrs. Ward and Dewey were . . . guilty of a drunken debauch with the convict women at night." The following morning, thirty of the female inmates were discovered in a drunken stupor. Investigators further reported, "There seems [sic] to be very well-grounded suspicions that licentious conduct between these two lessees and convict women was not unfrequent."[19]

Attempts to reform the penal system faced entrenched institutional and bureaucratic resistance from prison officials and guards. To make matters worse, rather than making surprise inspections, state investigators provided advance notice. Edward Anson Hart witnessed some of these inspections. When making inquiries as to prison conditions, the inspectors called "before them only such convicts as have become abject 'suckers' or lackeys to the sergeants, guards, or other bosses, only such convicts as the officers have in some devious ways bribed to lie for them."[20]

Hart recalled, "If any other convict should have the nerve to boldly make complaint, he is forthwith proven to be a liar by the bosses and all their 'suckers,' and when the committee or inspector leaves, he pays dearly for his boldness." Former inmate J. L. Wilkinson said prisoners learned to keep silent about the behavior of prison employees and their treatment of convicts. Inmates who spoke up risked "being beaten unmercifully, if not to death." Besides intimidating convicts, prison employees also menaced some of the inspectors. After Inspector J. K. P. Campbell reprimanded a guard named Welch for his brutal treatment of a prisoner, Welch told Campbell that "he hoped the next time a mutiny took place in the prison the convicts would cut my throat."[21]

In their final report to the Texas legislature, a special committee investigating prison conditions lamented that it was often difficult to ascertain the truth of what transpired inside the state facilities. Investigators found that the lessees "have much power over the convicts and are backed by a large body of hungry and in many cases, utterly unscrupulous guards and employees trembling at the possible loss of employment and often bound together by a cohesive power of a consciousness of crimes and cruelties jointly perpetrated." Summing up the situation, penal historian Donald Walker concluded, "The manner in which inmates in the Texas prison system [including Krebs, Preston, and Taylor] were treated during the late nineteenth and early twentieth centuries constituted a source of continuing shame for the state."[22]

Among the prison population during this period, only one-seventh had a trade or profession. Most prisoners were unskilled. Less than half of the convicts were Texas natives. Half the inmates were African American, 40 percent were white, and the remainder, Mexican (based on contemporary designations). Less than 2 percent was female. Most of the prisoners were thirty-five years of age or younger. Most used tobacco and more than half were drinkers. More than half were illiterate, while 40 percent had only limited education. Slightly less than one-third were married. The majority of convicts were serving sentences for burglary, robbery, and theft, including livestock theft. One-third of the population—including Krebs, Preston, and Taylor—was imprisoned for first- or second-degree murder, or assault with intent to murder. For the vast majority of inmates, this was their first incarceration in the state system. The leading cause of death inside the prison was consumption (tuberculosis), a very contagious disease.[23]

Every convict wore a prison uniform of either white-and-black or white-and-brown striped cloth. Summer dress included shoes, pants, shirt, and hat. In winter, prisoners wore shoes, socks, drawers, pants, jacket, and hat or cap. Winter jackets were lined and made of a half-wool, half-cloth blend. Painted on the back of every shirt was the convict's name, prison number, and a red or black ball. The red ball signified that the prisoner was a "lifer," while a black ball indicated a lesser punishment. One-tenth of the population, including Krebs, Preston, and Taylor were "red-ballers." Regulations stated that convicts should change their clothing once a week, or twice a week if dirty. Inmates washed their own laundry once a week with soap and water. Guards ensured that prisoners washed their faces daily, shaved once a week, kept their hair cut short, and bathed once a week in the summer and once every two weeks in the winter.[24]

Typically, two inmates shared a sparsely furnished cell that contained a stool and a bunkbed, with one man sleeping on the top bed, and the other on the lower. Mattresses and pillows were filled with corn husks and cotton, straw, moss, or hay. Each prisoner received two coarse striped sheets and a cotton comforter or blanket. Convicts changed their sheets once a week. When thirsty, the men could take their cups and fill them from a small water bucket that hung on a hook just outside the cell bars.[25]

Inmates rose at 5:30 each morning during the summer months and at 6:30 in the winter. After breakfast, the men marched off to their respective jobs. At Huntsville, prison industries included blacksmith, wagon, furniture, boiler, and machine shops; a brickyard; a cotton and wool factory; a tailor and mattress shop, a grist mill, a soap factory, and a laundry. Prisoners also worked as cooks, bakers, and hospital attendants. From December through February, convicts labored nine hours a day; during March, April, July, August, October, and November, ten hours; and during May, June, and September, eleven hours. Lights out was at 9 P.M.[26]

After serving almost two years of his life sentence, Aaron Kendrick Taylor died of dropsy, scurvy, and consumption at Huntsville on June 5, 1880. Texas State Prison Superintendent Thomas J. Goree visited the twenty-year-old Taylor "on his death bed." During the visit, Taylor swore to Goree that he, Krebs, and Preston were innocent and had had no part in the England family murders. When Taylor died, no one claimed his body so prison authorities buried him in a cheap pine coffin in a nondescript grave located in the northwest corner of the prison cemetery.[27]

Inmates called this graveyard "Peckerwood Hill," a corruption of the word "perkerwood," used to describe destitute or impoverished inmates. A wooden cross with Taylor's convict number, 6870, marked his otherwise anonymous resting place. A prison investigative committee appointed by the Texas legislature reported, "In many cases the graves were not over a few inches deep, sometimes the coffins had no lids, and in consequence of these two causes the hogs have on several occasions rooted up and scattered the bones of the dead." Almost a century later, prison workers replaced 312 of the cemetery's wooden markers (long since disintegrated) with concrete crosses. The exact location of Taylor's grave remains unknown because the state prison system did not start keeping cemetery records until 1974.[28]

On January 1, 1883, two and a half years after Aaron Taylor's death, guards transferred his brother-in-law Ben Krebs and James Preston to the state penitentiary located in the East Texas town of Rusk. Prison officials assigned Krebs and Preston new convict numbers, 347 and 348 respectively. Texas selected Rusk as the site for the prison in hopes of developing a profitable iron industry utilizing the region's large reserves of iron ore. The prison blast furnace became operational in February 1884 but was quickly beset by a number of problems. The furnace produced only one-third of the projected tonnage, and much of the iron proved to be substandard. It took the state almost two years to finally resolve these problems.[29]

In the biennial report on the Rusk prison in 1888, Assistant Superintendent William Neal Ramey noted that the prison population was 843. Ramey wrote that many of the "new convicts [were] undisciplined, of almost every character, embracing the worst in the state." According to the Texas Criminal Code, the primary purpose of incarceration was "to suppress crime and reform the offender," but Ramey's boss, Superintendent Goree, "reluctantly" confessed "that heretofore, not much has been accomplished towards the reformation of criminals in Texas."[30]

Ramey also reported, "Our punishment list has part of the time been very heavy as so many of the convicts of all types were thrown in together, many of whom were from jails where the discipline was bad and embracing old offenders whose experience enabled them to be instructors of the young and inexperienced and the stirrers up and originators of plots and schemes." One of these plots was a prison riot, which Ramey and his underkeeper, Captain Marion Ezell, succeeded in putting down. Within a year of making his 1888 report, Assistant Superintendent Ramey was forced to resign after officials discovered he had stolen almost $3,000 in funds held for the inmates at Rusk.[31]

Most of the convicts at Rusk worked in the prison's ironworks and foundries producing pig iron, water pipes, and general castings. Prisoners also labored at Rusk's tailor, blacksmith, shoe, harness, wagon, carpenter, paint, and machine shops. Apparently, the workforce left much to be desired. Superintendent Goree lamented, "There is a very large class of convicts in Texas . . . who are *totally* unfit for skilled labor and cannot be profitably employed." One inmate named Charles Campbell recalled working for several weeks as a coal tender at the pipe foundry. During his twelve-hour shift, he was confined in a "five-by-eight-foot space in front of the [boiling hot] furnaces and forced to shovel coal." Campbell said that he received no water during his shifts, and after two weeks of work, his blistered body resembled a cadaver. Campbell also asserted that he received no medical treatment for his injuries. Assessing the merits of the Rusk foundry, one writer remarked, "Truth be told, there wasn't much of a market for iron products in Texas. . . . In short, the largest iron manufactory of any kind in Texas amounted to, in the words of legislative investigators, a 'stupendous folly,' . . . [a] 'sinkhole for money.'"[32]

By 1885, Krebs and Preston had been incarcerated at the Rusk penitentiary for more than two years and had been in jail (either county or state) since August 1876. Reflecting upon their long, bleak years in prison, the two men likely felt hopeless, that they and their steadfast protestations of innocence had been long forgotten. This was not the case, however. In 1885, five years after he had commuted their death sentences to life at hard labor, the now former governor Oran Milo Roberts was still thinking about the England murders. In early May of that year, Roberts visited with the Dallas legal firm of Crawford & Crawford to discuss the cases of Ben Krebs and James Preston.[33]

— 7 —

Former governor O. M. Roberts met with the Dallas legal firm in May 1885 for the purpose of exploring pardons for Ben Krebs and James Preston. Following the visit, a representative of Crawford & Crawford wrote to Roberts, informing him that they had discussed the former governor's proposal with a number of concerned persons. These people had expressed their sincere appreciation for Roberts's interest and offered their assistance in lobbying the current governor on behalf of Krebs and Preston.[1]

The attorneys advised Roberts that if he would put together a pardon application to present to his successor, Gov. John Ireland, they would then circulate a pardon petition and secure the requisite number of signatures from influential Texans. Four days later, Joseph Alexander Carroll, the former district judge who had presided over all five trials of Ben Krebs, James Preston, and Aaron Taylor, wrote to Roberts. Carroll had heard Roberts wanted "to make an effort to. . . . [effect] the pardon of Krebs and Preston" and wrote "I desire to say that I will at any time join you in the effort."[2]

Securing pardons would be no easy matter, especially in light of the views of Governor Ireland. Ireland, who succeeded Roberts in 1882, had capitalized on the backlash over the Krebs-Preston commutations while campaigning for governor. Ireland's platform included severe criticism of the excessive use of executive clemency by Texas governors. Roberts's commutations had angered many in Texas, including his own attorney general, George McCormick. McCormick was so incensed that he declined to run for re-election with Roberts in 1880. The attorney general visited "the old alcalde [a popular nickname for Roberts] and with his characteristic candor he notified him that Texas was going to hell under such a policy. Then it was that the alcalde made the celebrated response: 'Let her go; it's according to the law.'"[3]

Roberts might have followed the law, but his actions had poisoned the well for controversial pardons in the short term, and especially for notorious convicts such as Krebs and Preston. Ultimately, Roberts's pardon inquiries fizzled out. Governor Ireland proved unreceptive. According to one account, during Ireland's tenure in office (1882–86) he "urged a persistent enforcement of criminal laws and reduced the number of pardons." Perhaps this was true for the overall number of pardons Ireland issued, but an examination of his pardon registers for murder convictions tells a different story.[4]

Like Roberts, Ireland commuted ten murder in the first degree death sentences to life in prison. Regarding life sentences for murder, Ireland pardoned twenty-five individuals, more than two and a half times Roberts's record. What is more, Ireland took the rare step of pardoning someone sentenced to death for murder in the first degree, something Roberts never did. In any case, after Roberts's pardon efforts failed to gain traction with Ireland in 1885, he transitioned from being point person to assisting other concerned parties advocating for Krebs and Preston.[5]

In the fall of 1887, relatives of James Preston hired Dallas attorney W. C. Wolff to lobby John Ireland's successor, Gov. Lawrence Sullivan "Sul" Ross, to pardon Krebs and Preston. In September, Wolff initiated his outreach to Ross. Wolff pointed out to the governor that former Judge Carroll endorsed pardoning both men. Former Governor Roberts had commuted their death sentences in 1880, and since then had supported their pardons. Wolff told Ross, "Governor Roberts did not believe them guilty, he could not, and has always said so, and he would have pardoned them at once had he not thought it better for their safety to keep them in confinement a while longer, to save them from mob violence." In addition, Wolff informed Ross that more than one hundred citizens of Montague County who lived near the England murder site favored pardoning the two men.[6]

In opposition to Wolff's efforts, former state district attorney Finis Piner, who had helped prosecute the England murders, started a petition drive against the pardons. Piner had been incensed at Governor Roberts for commuting Krebs's and Preston's sentences and had endeavored to sabotage Roberts's 1880 re-election. Piner, who had since succeeded Joseph A. Carroll as district judge for the Sixteenth

Judicial District, sent his petition to Governor Ross in early October 1887. The signatories believed that the two men should have been executed in 1880. Several elected officials from Montague County signed Piner's petition opposing the pardons, including the county judge, county attorney, county sheriff, county treasurer, county clerk, district court clerk, and justice of the peace.[7]

Wolff persisted however, and over the next several months, he forwarded Governor Ross additional documents, petitions, and letters from people who supported the pardons. In September, Thomas J. Goree, superintendent of the Texas State Prisons, penned two Prison Conduct Certificates at Governor Ross's request, one for Krebs, the other for Preston. Goree reported that since Krebs had entered the prison system his comportment had been spotless, without one black mark against him. James Preston's behavior had also been excellent, with no infractions of prison regulations. In addition, Goree mentioned the deathbed conversation he had with Aaron Taylor in early June 1880. He said that Taylor had "protested the innocence of all three of the crime for which convicted" and declared "on his deathbed a few days before his death, that he and Krebs and Preston were guiltless of the crime for which convicted and had nothing to do with it whatsoever."[8]

On September 5, 1887, Mrs. Luna Dickerson, the former wife of John R. Music, wrote to Governor Ross to advocate for pardoning Krebs and Preston. Luna told Ross that she had been contacted by relatives of Preston's, asking her to write a letter of support. Luna said that on the night of the murders, she and her husband had taken Selena England into their home, and that she had stayed with Selena continually until she died the following day. Luna stated that Selena never accused Preston, whom she knew well, of being involved in the killings. Luna further stated that Harvey Taylor, who had since died, never implicated Krebs, Preston, or Aaron Taylor in the slayings. Instead, Harvey told Luna that "Bill Taylor was one [of the murderers], and that . . . Mr. Music, pointing at him, he thought was the other. . . . [In addition,] Mr. Music had been hunting hogs with Bill Taylor the day the murder[s] occurred."[9]

Luna concluded her letter to Governor Ross by noting, "Harvey always contended that Bill Taylor was one of the parties. Bill Taylor left this country at the time and has never returned to my knowledge. Mr. Music left here sometimes [sic] afterwards, I am divorced from him and have married again. I have never thought Harvey Taylor a fool, yet he had crazy spells, I was told this was caused by studying the Bible too much." Luna said that she favored giving Krebs and Preston a full pardon, and argued that most of the local hostility and ill will against the two men had faded. Luna was certain that 90 percent of Montague County would sign a pardon petition.[10]

On October 7, 1887, J. W. Wayburn, the new acting deputy sheriff of Montague County, drafted a statement to Governor Ross. Wayburn said that he had first met Krebs early in the Civil War and had known James Preston for about two years prior to the murders. In addition, he had been around Aaron Taylor since he was a baby and was well acquainted with one of his sisters, Margaret Taylor Patrick. According to Wayburn, Margaret "tried to get her brother A. K. Taylor to turn state's evidence and to say that Preston and Krebs were guilty, but . . . he refused, saying he would rather die in the penitentiary than to swear falsely, for he knew nothing to swear, and that so far as he [knew], neither Krebs [n]or Preston had anything to do with the murder of the England Family."[11]

Wayburn said that Margaret pressured her brother to swear the two were guilty anyway, even if it was false, to save his own skin, but Aaron refused. The deputy sheriff recalled that during the quarter century he had known Krebs, the latter had always been a hardworking, peaceable man. Although Wayburn did not know Preston well, he observed that he could be both feisty and scrappy when drinking, "but very quiet and gentlemanly when sober and a good neighbor from report." Apparently, the deputy sheriff had originally intended to include the crossed-out phrase in his statement but removed it upon further reflection.[12]

In early November 1887, attorney W. C. Wolff wrote again to Governor Ross regarding pardons and the Texas legal system. Wolff observed that it appeared executive clemency was not currently in vogue. Wolff understood that judges and courts were often wary of overturning jury verdicts because of the public perception that the judgment of twelve men was superior to that of one. Although this view might deter some judges from taking action, Wolff felt that the governor had much more leeway in exercising executive clemency.[13]

Wolff pointed out that in the England murder case, Montague County Attorney Avery Lenoir Matlock had ginned up local opinion against Krebs and Preston to "a fever heat." Particularly because Matlock lived in the county seat of Montague, his influence proved considerable "in molding popular sentiment against the accused." In the face of such pressure, Wolff doubted that anyone could receive a fair trial. He closed his letter with an emotional appeal to Governor Ross that he hoped that "the poor old innocent men" would be freed so that they could return to their families before they died. Wolff had recently seen "old Mrs. [Rhoda] Krebs as I was going on the stage from Bowie to Montague, the old lady cried when I told her the object of my mission. She said, 'God knows they are not guilty.'" Wolff said that although Krebs's and Preston's children were impoverished, they were respectable and would give all they had, "which is only a few cows and ponies, to see their dear papas."[14]

In mid-November, Lucas F. Smith, a member of the legal team that had helped defend James Preston, wrote to Governor Ross. Reviewing the England family murders, he pointed out that Harvey Taylor, the sole surviving witness to the carnage, was now deceased. Harvey had been lying on the porch when the three killers approached the house. The moon was bright that night and Harvey had good eyesight. "The murderer had every opportunity to kill him," Smith said, "yet strange to say . . . never attempted it. This shows that the murderer had some ill feelings towards the four persons murdered and not against Harvey."[15]

During Preston's trial at Gainesville, Harvey Taylor had told Smith and co-counsel James Mann Hurt "that he knew the defendants were not the men who did the murder. He called upon God to witness the truth of the assertion." Smith asked Harvey why, if this was the case, had he not said so in his testimony during Aaron Taylor's trial? Harvey replied "he was afraid the people [vigilantes] would kill him, as they had threatened his life unless he testified the defendants were the ones. And the poor fellow was so harassed and threatened that he had to leave Montague County and go to Gordonsville in Grayson County, where he died one or two years ago." During his testimony, Harvey had stated that the killers were about the same size as Krebs and Preston. Harvey later told Smith and Hurt that he said this "to save his life from threatened danger." In his closing remarks to Ross, Smith said he was "hoping and praying that both Krebs and Preston may be pardoned by your excellency."[16]

As 1887 drew to a close, W. C. Wolff wrote one last letter to Governor Ross. Wolff expressed appreciation for the consideration that Ross had extended to him during the past year in his efforts to secure pardons for Krebs and Preston. He reported Preston's relatives had hired him to work on their behalf only until the new year. Recognizing that by now the governor had likely reached a decision, Wolff stated that he hoped his efforts had not been in vain.[17]

At the bottom of Wolff's last letter is a handwritten postscript by Governor Ross, "After long and thorough examination of this whole case I cannot see my way clear to interfere in behalf of Preston & Cribs [sic]." In comparison to O. M. Roberts's and John Ireland's executive clemency records, Sul Ross's pardon registers reveal that he was more conservative. During his two terms, he commuted seven death sentences for murder in the first degree to life in prison, while pardoning nine individuals sentenced to life sentences for murder. Despite the compelling evidence surfacing in the England murder case, two Texas governors—first John Ireland then Sul Ross—refused to get involved. At this point, Krebs and Preston had been incarcerated for more than eleven years.[18]

Two years later, in March 1890, James Preston penned a letter to former governor O. M. Roberts, asking for help in rekindling interest in a pardon. Preston expressed his gratitude to Roberts for being his "most reliable friend," for acting on behalf of an innocent man, and for standing firm amidst the considerable backlash and bitter denunciations generated by his commutations. He then asked Roberts for his frank opinion regarding the likelihood of a pardon. Did the former governor consider his situation hopeless? Preston said that knowing his prospects was preferable to living a life in constant uncertainty, swinging back and forth between hope and fear. "It is a fearful thing for a man to consent to die in prison for something he never did," Preston wrote, "and knowing there is others that knows he is innocent."[19]

Upon receipt of Preston's letter, Roberts forwarded it to Governor Ross with an attached note. Roberts told Ross that he was sorry to bother him but, "The old man in the penitentiary keeps writing to me as if I had some power to give him some relief." Roberts said that he firmly believed Preston and Krebs to be innocent since no new evidence had come to light which would lead him to judge otherwise. Preston's and Roberts's letters failed to change Ross's mind. Once again, the governor took no action in the matter.[20]

By 1891, Ross had been succeeded by a new governor, James Stephen Hogg. In November of that year, James Preston reached out to Hogg directly to plead his case anew. Preston's letter to Hogg was given considerable gravitas by the person who forwarded it to the governor, Elbridge Geary Douglass, assistant superintendent of Rusk Penitentiary where Preston and Krebs were incarcerated. Douglass added his own endorsement to Preston's letter, asking the governor to read it carefully because he considered every word in it to be accurate. He told Hogg that he had been at Krebs's trial and that ever since, had firmly believed in both Krebs's and Preston's innocence. Douglass had always regretted the years of suffering that both men were forced to endure. Krebs's and Preston's convictions "were the result of high excitement and public clamor for some sacrifice to an exasperated community in the heat of which the merest circumstance of suspicion was deemed sufficient," Douglass continued, and "all the long years since that day have strengthened my conviction of their innocence."[21]

Preston's letter to Hogg followed Douglass's endorsement:

After fifteen long, weary, and miserable years, waiting in the hope and belief that time would right the great wrong that has been done me, after spending the accumulation of almost a lifetime of honest toil in the effort to bring my grievances before the chief executive of our state in such a manner that he would see, know, and feel the truths, after my head is whitened and bowed by time and suffering, I come to you sir, while on the brink of my grave, and beg you spare me one moment while I write to you as truthful and pitiful a history as was ever the misfortune of man to hear. . . . Before my God and you I come today and swear that I am an innocent man. That my conviction was due solely to the fact that prejudice existed against me to such an extent that my enemies swore away my life and liberty, there is no question that I was tried and convicted by men that had proposed to help lynch me and after that, could help answer all the questions to make them legal jurors, and [by] men who were organized and powerful to do in the community as they pleased [i.e., County Attorney Matlock]. I am an old man and there remains for me at best, a very few short years of life. God in heaven knows that I am innocent of the crime for which I suffer. But what am I to do, penniless and . . . forgotten by them who knew and honored me when my name was spotless, I have no recourse but through you, no hope but that God will direct you and bring the truth to light.[22]

Whereas previous appeals to John Ireland and Sul Ross had fallen on deaf ears, in Hogg they found a receptive audience. The new governor began studying the Krebs-Preston pardon file in earnest. Then, eight months after Douglass and Preston made their outreach to Hogg, events in the England murder case took a major turn. On July 20, 1892, Luna Dickerson, former wife of John Music, substantially augmented her previous statements in a new affidavit sworn at Montague, Texas. As with Harvey Taylor's courtroom testimony, one can read between the lines and sense that for years, Luna had withheld what she knew regarding the England murders because she feared for her own and her children's safety. For many people involved in the case, the specters of vigilante intimidation and violent retribution were always hovering nearby.[23]

Luna started off her new affidavit by stating that she did not personally know who killed the England family. With that said, it soon became clear she had a fairly good idea who several of the murderers were. "But I do know that Mr. [John R.] Music who was then my husband was accused of being implicated in the murders of said England family and immediately after the murder was done Mr. Music began to wind up his business and as soon as that was done he left the country." John Music's departure suggests he had a guilty conscience. In 1877, the year following the slayings, Music left Montague County and relocated the family to Jack County. Then he moved them to Wise County. Next, he decided to go to Mexico, stopping in Llano County on his way south. Luna said her husband "seemed to get very uneasy" in Llano County and soon changed his mind yet again. He left Llano County and returned to Wise County, whereupon he abandoned Luna and their children.[24]

Luna said that her husband always seemed reluctant to discuss the England case. He "did tell me one day soon after the murder[s] that there was a [pistol] ball found imbedded in a chest in the England house the next morning after the killing . . . that was shot out of a gun that he had in his hands the day before" the killings. Since this gun was never found, John Music did not mention it to anyone. He also told Luna that he and Bill Taylor had spent time together on the day of the murders. As to John's motives for possibly harming the Englands, Luna explained, "There was an old grudge existing between the England family and Mr. Music on account of a piece of land that Mr. Music claimed his father had preempted and that the land belonged to Mr. Music but the England family had settled on the land and would not give it up."[25]

As previously mentioned, Music's father, William Granville Music, had originally intended to homestead the Thomas N. Savage Survey that Selena England later purchased. On October 20, 1860, William Music had the acreage surveyed, but he failed to live there for three consecutive years as required by Texas homestead law. By 1868, the State of Texas considered the land vacant and Thomas N. Savage settled on it. On June 15, 1871, after Savage homesteaded the land, the Texas General Land Office issued him a patented title to the 160 acres. Savage subsequently sold the property. Montague County tax rolls show that in 1875, Selena England was the legal owner of the Savage Survey. Nonetheless, John Music still harbored a bitter resentment against the Englands, and especially against Selena England.[26]

Luna recalled a number of occasions when Selena had uttered cruel taunts about the Savage Survey, telling "Mr. Music that if he had any money, he had better save it, and that she had plenty of money and would see that he never would be able to beat her out of the place, and of course Mr. Music did not like that one bit." On the night of the murders, Luna had already gone to sleep when her husband returned home. He announced that he would get a straw mattress and sleep in the doorway, which was unusual considering that he always slept in their bed.[27]

Later that night, after the wounded Selena had crawled to the Music home for aid, Selena's son Harvey Taylor came to visit her. Luna was present in the room when Harvey was talking to his mother. Selena asked Harvey if he knew "who the parties were that did the shooting (as he was on the porch when they drew their pistols and began shooting)." Harvey said yes, one of the killers was Bill Taylor and another was John Music. Luna recalled that when Harvey named Music, Selena responded, "'Hush, Mr. Music is here [in another room],' and then Harvey said, 'it was a small man with [a] red beard and looked just like Mr. Music.'" With her new affidavit, Luna Dickerson had just reopened the England murder case.[28]

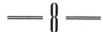

Luna Dickerson's July 1892 affidavit seriously compromised Ben Krebs's and James Preston's murder convictions. Sensing an opening, James Preston's relatives in Montague County began lobbying Gov. James S. Hogg for a pardon. Hogg was now the fourth chief executive of Texas to be linked to the England murder case. On August 1, 1892, Montague attorney William James Sparks forwarded Luna's affidavit to Governor Hogg along with a petition signed by two hundred people asking the governor to pardon James Preston. Sparks had been part of the defense team for both Ben Krebs's and James Preston's appeals in 1880.[1]

In a note accompanying the petition, Sparks wrote that throughout his involvement in the case, he had always believed Preston to be innocent. Luna's affidavit confirmed what his gut had long told him: John Music and Bill Taylor were two of the murderers, "neither of whom was suspected except by Harvey Taylor, a weakminded boy who escaped and was the only eyewitness who testified." Sparks's petition noted that there was much fear and panic in the region following the brutal murders and that some people jumped to erroneous conclusions.[2]

In early August, prominent Austin attorney and former Texas attorney general William Martin Walton wrote to the governor, adding his unequivocal support for pardoning Preston. Walton reported that his careful review of the trial transcript raised serious questions regarding Preston's involvement. In addition, Luna Dickerson's recent affidavit "makes it more than probable that the innocent are undergoing punishment while the guilty one is now at large in liberty." During the same week in August, former Montague County judge Griffin Ford also penned a letter to Hogg. Ford had previously signed Finis Piner's 1887 petition to Gov. Sul Ross recommending against a pardon. Since then, Ford had clearly had a change of heart. The former judge, who had been familiar with the case since 1876, pointed out in his letter to Hogg that much of the evidence upon which Krebs and Preston were convicted was circumstantial in nature. Moreover, "The enthusiasm injected into the case by A. L. Matlock, prosecuting [county] attorney, went a long way toward conviction."[3]

Despite significant developments in the England murder case and growing support for pardons, Governor Hogg refused to be rushed into a decision. He would carefully consider the matter. As 1892 drew to a close, Ben Krebs's twenty-two-year-old daughter Annie mailed a letter to Governor Hogg. By this time, the Krebs family had moved from Montague County and were living in Lone Grove, Indian Territory, near present-day Ardmore, Oklahoma. During Krebs's many years in prison, his wife, Rhoda, and their children had been forced to fend for themselves.[4]

Annie Krebs, a young woman who exhibited grit and integrity, divided her long days between working in the fields and tending house. According to one report, she had "educated herself to a surprising degree" and was clearly not the child of a murderer. The head of the Krebs household, Rhoda, like many people during this period, could not read or write, so Annie served as the family scribe. In her letter to Governor Hogg, she inquired whether he had been able to review her father's file. She averred that Hogg would understand her writing to him and would sympathize with a child pleading for the release of her beloved father. "More especially," Annie wrote, "when that father is innocent of a crime, he has been a prisoner now for sixteen years and that punishment has fallen equally as heavy on members of his family as on himself."[5]

Annie reminded the governor that Christmas, the anniversary of Jesus's birth, was fast approaching. She asked Hogg to think of her on December 25, "on my knees with uplifted hands begging for the restoration to us of our dear old father so long shut off from life's opportunities." She then reflected upon the many Christmases that had come and gone since her father had been sent to prison, and each year the family hoping and praying that the next one would see their father back home, celebrating the holidays with them. Annie implored Hogg, "Oh, brighten some soon coming future day for us will you, can you, . . . may God above whisper to your heart all else that I would say."[6]

Governor Hogg did not reply to Annie Krebs, leading her to pen a follow-up letter during the summer of 1893. This time she sent the letter, along with an attached note, in care of former Texas governor Francis Richard Lubbock. In 1891, Hogg had appointed Lubbock and Judge L. D. Brooks to oversee the Texas Board of Pardon Advisers. The two-man board assisted the governor with his ever-increasing workload by evaluating potential pardons and making recommendations. Lubbock, who had served as Texas's chief executive from 1861 to 1863, was now the fifth governor to become involved in the England murder case. "Dear sir, no doubt you will be surprised at reading a letter from a poor girl a way out in the Chickasaw Nation," Annie wrote Lubbock, "enclosed . . . you will find a letter I have written to Governor Hogg in behalf of my father Ben Krebs who has been a poor prisoner deprived of his liberty now for sixteen years." Annie continued, "I trust to God that you will be interested enough to do some favorable action for us and our dear good father and husband."[7]

The day after Annie composed her letter, Ben Krebs's former cellmate joined the chorus of those clamoring for his release. On July 26, O. P. Taylor, who had bunked with Krebs at Rusk, wrote to the Board of Pardons. In his note, Taylor remarked that he had been a prisoner at Rusk for almost two years, starting in 1891. During his time there he had come to know Krebs well and considered him an exemplary person. According to Taylor, Krebs was a wonderful family man and a devoted father and husband. Krebs loved "children, pets, and flowers. Does God vouchsafe these attributes to such as are capable of murdering a whole family?" Taylor added, "He sleeps like a man with a clear conscience. A brutal man can sleep with the blood of the victim fresh upon him. No man of his sensitiveness could." While Krebs's prison record at Rusk was in fact exemplary, one cannot take Taylor's facile, one-dimensional portrait at face value. Krebs, like most humans, was multifaceted. One must evaluate his conduct both while incarcerated and during the summer of 1876; specifically, his public threats about killing William and Selena England, and "cleaning up" Selena's son, Isaiah.[8]

Perhaps the most significant part of O. P. Taylor's letter to the Board of Pardons was a conversation he claimed to have overheard between two inmates at Rusk. Allegedly, one prisoner told the other he was certain that Krebs was not involved in the England murders. The convict said he knew this because Bill Taylor and his confederates had stopped at his house for breakfast the morning after the killings. Taylor told him over breakfast, "in the presence of his wife, that they had just killed these people."[9]

By early August 1893, both Krebs and Preston had made formal pardon applications to Governor Hogg. On August 10, Marion Ezell, prison underkeeper at Rusk, wrote a letter to Hogg. This was the same Marion Ezell whom a number of convicts had called a brutal sadist and a bane to their existence. Ezell told Hogg that for much of the time that Krebs and Preston had been at Huntsville (1880–82), and at Rusk (1883–93), they had been under his direct supervision. Ezell said that never once during their incarceration had he or a guard had reason to chastise them for misconduct. Both men had served as prison trustees for years and had always been diligent in their work. Then, in a truly remarkable statement given Ezell's notorious reputation among inmates he wrote, "These are the first men during my twenty-three-years [of] experience in the convict business I have ever recommended for pardon and I do so upon the grounds of their exceptionally good prison record and long servitude, be they innocent or be they guilty, the ends of justice have been fully met." For those within the Texas prison system, Marion Ezell advocating a pardon was indeed something to take notice of. Ezell's letter was yet another notable development in a case that seventeen years on, continued to surprise.[10]

Also during the month of August the Texas Board of Pardon Advisers began compiling pardon files on Krebs and Preston. Three months later, in November 1893, board members Francis Richard Lubbock and Judge L. D. Brooks mailed letters to a number of people, soliciting their opinion on whether Krebs and Preston should be pardoned. The first to respond was former Texas governor Oran Milo Roberts. In his inquiry to Roberts, Judge Brooks had asked him to state his reasons for commuting Krebs's and Preston's death sentences to life in prison rather than pardoning them outright. The former governor replied that in 1880 the issue was not whether to pardon them, but whether to hang them or to commute their sentences to life at hard labor.[11]

Roberts reminded Brooks that District Judge J. A. Carroll had requested commutations, not pardons, for Krebs and Preston. The judge told Roberts that he harbored grave reservations about their guilt. Since Carroll, the presiding judge over all five trials, had asked him to commute their sentences, Roberts was comfortable granting his request. In reviewing the England murders, the former governor noted that Krebs was convicted largely on Selena England's dying declarations. Other evidence in the case, however, had raised considerable uncertainty about Krebs's involvement. Roberts believed that the two men were "innocent beyond a reasonable doubt" and that juror bias against the defendants had negatively influenced the verdicts. He stated that he never considered pardoning Krebs and Preston because even though "I thought the fact that they were the guilty parties was very improbable, still to have pardoned them I would have had to given as a reason for it that I was satisfied from the conflicting evidence that they were innocent beyond a reasonable doubt."[12]

Roberts then indirectly referenced a point previously raised in 1880 by the Court of Appeals and others, that overturning jury verdicts eroded citizens' trust in Texas's legal system and thereby encouraged frustrated vigilante groups to take the law into their own hands. He felt that in the England case, he should be prudent and show proper deference for the decision of the juries and courts. Therefore, the former governor believed that the correct course of action was first to commute their sentences to life, then to hold off on further action until new developments arose in the case to confirm either their innocence or their guilt.[13]

Roberts said he thought that in time, it was possible that Krebs and Preston might be pardoned, but he does not mention when that time might be. Ten years? Twenty years? When they were dead? If indeed the two men were innocent, was it morally right that they should wither away in prison at hard labor until some future Texas governor finally found the fortitude to take action? Ultimately, when one reads between the lines here, it seems clear that while Roberts had doubts as to Krebs's and Preston's guilt in 1880, he was also not certain of their innocence.[14]

Roberts then presented an additional justification for his decision; namely, that he did not pardon the two men in order to protect them from harm. He pointed out to Brooks that not only were Krebs and Preston "tried under the strongest prejudice against them," their lives were also in serious danger from a vigilante attack. The former governor stated that he took extra security measures to have the two men moved from the Gainesville jail to the state penitentiary before they were scheduled to be executed. He noted that this precaution proved to be wise because after locals learned of the commutations more than two hundred citizens from Montague County converged on Gainesville to lynch them.[15]

Roberts said, "I was apprehensive of their safety from violence, even while in custody of the [Gainesville] officers, and of course there would have been much greater violence to them if they had been set at liberty, which was fully verified on the day appointed for their execution." If one follows this reasoning, then Roberts sent Krebs and Preston to life at hard labor for their own good, to keep them safe from vigilantes. This once again begs the question of time. How long would it be before they were out of harm's way? Ten years? Twenty years? When they were dead? Roberts did not address this issue.[16]

Deflecting once again, Roberts said that ultimately these points no longer mattered. The present issue was not whether he should have issued commutations or pardons in 1880, but whether these two old men should spend their remaining time on earth behind bars, before facing their divine judgment. Despite Roberts's equivocal explanations, it seems clear that the real reason he never pardoned Krebs and Preston is that he did not want to be blamed if it turned out that they were in fact guilty of the England murders. By keeping them in prison for life, he tried to effect a compromise, saving them from death if they were innocent and protecting the public if they were not. Roberts's unsatisfactory compromise did not resolve the issue, it only delayed resolution, and at Krebs's and Preston's expense.[17]

The Board of Pardon Advisers also received feedback from James P. Gibson, assistant superintendent of the Rusk Penitentiary. On November 25, 1893, Gibson wrote to board member F. R. Lubbock. Gibson reported that his predecessor at Rusk, Capt. Elbridge Geary Douglass, was very familiar with both prisoners and believed them to be innocent. Gibson said that while he had been at Rusk, he had studied the character of both men and talked with them on many occasions, leading him to form the same conclusion as Douglass. The assistant superintendent noted that during their thirteen years at Huntsville and Rusk "neither has ever made an attempt to escape or resist prison authority. Both have always performed, cheerfully, the duties to which they have been assigned, and have in all things been faithful, obedient, industrious, and respectful to officials and guards."[18]

The next day, November 26, Gibson sent Lubbock a follow-up letter containing a most remarkable testimonial. The assistant superintendent wrote, "I desire to say that in addition to what I wrote you yesterday, *that there were about ninety guards and employees connected with this prison, some of whom have been connected with prison management ever since Krebs and Preston have been in the penitentiary, and that there is not one but what believes in their innocence. . . .* If you think it necessary or will do any good in any way, every attaché of this prison in an official capacity will sign a petition in their belief in the innocence of Krebs and Preston and ask for their pardon" (emphasis added). This is an extremely unusual and rare occurrence in the annals of Texas prison history for more than ninety prison employees to volunteer to sign a pardon petition declaring their belief in the innocence of two men convicted by multiple juries of slaughtering a family. Gibson's statement is yet another extraordinary aspect of this case. The assistant superintendent closed his letter to Lubbock by voicing his belief that anyone who observed the two men on a daily basis would see firsthand their excellent conduct and steadfast obedience to prison regulations and would be persuaded that they were not the kind of men who would commit murder.[19]

During the fall of 1893 Governor Hogg traveled to the state penitentiary at Rusk and visited Ben Krebs. The fact that Hogg would pay Krebs a visit was a clear indicator that the ground was now shifting and momentum for a pardon was gaining traction, albeit slowly. On December 17, Hogg requested that Judge L. D. Brooks and former governor F. R. Lubbock, as his pardon advisers, make a thorough examination of the Krebs and Preston cases and report their findings. On December 23, Brooks and Lubbock forwarded their conclusions and recommendations to Hogg.[20]

Brooks and Lubbock started their review of the case by noting that Krebs and Preston were convicted largely on the dying declarations of Selena England. Selena's son, Harvey, knew both Krebs and Preston, yet he identified the pistol-brandishing, mustached young man who came within two or three feet of him on the porch as Bill Taylor. Harvey also recognized a second man, who stopped at the gate, as John Music. Selena had told Krebs in the presence of County Attorney Avery Matlock that she recognized Krebs from his hat and beard as Isaiah Taylor's murderer and the man who had chased her and her daughter Susie. Harvey, however, described this man as having a mustache, not a beard, and as wearing not a hat but a rag tied around his head.[21]

Brooks and Lubbock next criticized Matlock's methods, saying that the young county attorney had placed too much importance upon the three sets of tracks that he had found leading from the England home to within fifty yards of the Krebs cabin. The advisers acknowledged that criminals sometimes did stupid things that later incriminated them, but it was nonetheless hard to believe that if Krebs, Preston, and Aaron Taylor were indeed the murderers, they would be stupid enough to walk straight back to the Krebs home through recently plowed fields, leaving their tracks for all to see. Brooks and Lubbock offered an alternative scenario. One of the killers knew that both Susie and Selena Taylor suspected Krebs of being the man who pursued them, firing his pistol, because Susie called out Krebs's name several times during the pursuit. The murderers may have deliberately tried to cast further suspicion on Krebs by walking directly from the England home across the plowed fields toward the Krebs home.[22]

Brooks and Lubbock also noted it was significant that the murderers did not kill Selena England. If Ben Krebs were one of her attackers, why would he not have finished her off, silencing her forever, instead of just wounding her, leaving her alive to identify him as her murderer? It was plausible the killers deliberately chose not to kill her so that she would implicate Krebs and thus divert suspicion from them. That Krebs would leave Selena to identify him then would head straight home across freshly turned earth, leaving a clear, incriminating trail seemed doubly ludicrous. The advisers asked, "Does this conduct comport with our knowledge and observation of criminals trying to hide the evidence of their crime, . . . or rather, is it not flatly contra to all our knowledge and observation on the subject?"[23]

After pointing out how ridiculous such a scenario was, Brooks and Lubbock then zeroed in on a more likely explanation: that the killers wanted to frame Ben Krebs for the murders. Common sense dictated that if Krebs, Preston, and Taylor had been the guilty parties, they would have taken a far different, more discreet route when returning to the Krebs home, and would have been more careful of leaving incriminating footprints. The advisers next addressed the nature of the offense, a "wholesale indiscriminate and cowardly butchery of an inoffensive, helpless family, [a crime that was] . . . well calculated to arouse and did arouse even to frenzy, the righteous indignation of that outraged community to the degree of intensity that the people, in their eagerness and determination to punish the perpetrators of that appalling crime, were incapable of considering dispassionately the facts and circumstances that seemed to them at the time to point to these men as the guilty perpetrators of this great crime."[24]

Brooks and Lubbock noted that it was common in the heat of the moment for individuals to jettison a calm and rational perspective and jump to conclusions, seizing upon convenient facts that appeared incriminating while ignoring other equally valid evidence that might exonerate a suspect. People see what they want to see. Often in a rush to judgment, suspicion is focused on innocent parties, allowing the guilty to escape justice. The advisers concluded, "There existed against these men at the time of their trials such an inflamed state of passion and prejudice as to make it impossible for them to have a fair and impartial trial."[25]

Brooks and Lubbock did not believe that Krebs and Preston were "the vile and bloody demons that the crime for which they were convicted would indicate, [as] is clearly established by the statements of prison officials . . . who have had them in [their] charge these many long years." In summary, Brooks and Lubbock wrote "these men are the unfortunate victims of a combination of circumstances, prejudice, and passion, and are being punished for the crimes of other men, [and] we recommend their immediate pardon and their restoration to full citizenship."[26]

Despite the board's recommendation, 1893 would end with no executive clemency for Krebs and Preston. As the pages of the calendar kept turning, Governor Hogg was determined to take his time in carefully examining all aspects of the England murders. He would not be rushed into making a hasty and ill-informed decision in a case long steeped in considerable controversy and political liability.

$$=9=$$

For much of 1894, little was heard of Krebs and Preston, or of a pardon from Governor Hogg. Hogg was now a lame duck serving his last year in office. On November 6, 1894, Texas Attorney General Charles Allen Culberson won the election to succeed Hogg. Culberson's term would start on January 15, 1895. If Hogg had opted to run for the U.S. Senate in 1896, he likely would have won, but he chose instead to resume his private law practice.[1]

In hindsight, perhaps Hogg decided not to take any decisive action on Krebs and Preston until he decided his future plans for elected office. On October 17, 1894, three weeks before Election Day, Hogg launched a new and confidential investigation into the England family murders. He hired Elbridge Geary Douglass, former state senator from Grayson and Cooke Counties and former assistant superintendent of the Rusk Prison, to make some discreet inquiries in Montague County. Douglass, it may be recalled, knew Krebs and Preston from his time at Rusk and was always a steadfast believer in their innocence.[2]

Hogg instructed Douglass to try and establish Bill Taylor's whereabouts in Montague County during the time of the murders. Several eyewitnesses had reported seeing Taylor in the area prior to the killings. Douglass proceeded to Montague County and after canvassing area residents, found a father and son who had observed Bill Taylor riding toward the England home two days before the murders. The two men, father Robert Allen McGrady and son Charles Frank

McGrady, talked freely with Douglass about meeting Taylor. The son signed an affidavit for Douglass stating that on the afternoon of Thursday, August 24, he and his father saw Bill Taylor and another man crossing Clear Creek in Montague County on the road leading toward the England residence. The McGradys were standing in the bed of Clear Creek when Taylor and his associate rode by them.[3]

In conversing with a county official, Douglass learned that the McGradys were well-known, established farmers and honest, upstanding citizens. He also discovered a sea change in local opinion regarding the perpetrators of the England murders. The vast majority of county residents now believed that Bill Taylor had been one of the killers. During Douglass's visit to Montague, District Clerk W. A. Morris told him that Bill Taylor had been indicted in district court on March 17, 1875 for horse theft and was a fugitive from justice at the time of the England murders. Regarding Krebs's and Preston's reputations locally, Douglass reported that he could not find one person who had anything bad to say about Krebs. Many described him as a trustworthy and valued citizen, and some referenced his tenure as Montague County district clerk as evidence of his standing in the community. As for Preston, the only derogatory thing Douglass heard about him was that he had a predilection for spiritous liquors and fisticuffs.[4]

Douglass told Governor Hogg that he had originally intended to conduct a circumspect investigation into the England case, but he soon found that everyone knew his business. He told folks that he was there gathering evidence for the defense that was not included in the original trial, evidence that was suppressed on account of the intense anger, fear, and prejudice that raged throughout North Texas following the England murders. During his twelve days in Montague County, Douglass learned that for many years, people who had relevant information had been fearful of speaking up. Locals were now more willing to share what they knew.[5]

In his closing remarks to the governor, Douglass estimated that 80 percent of county residents would sign a petition to pardon Krebs and Preston. Regarding Bill Taylor, he said that during August 1876, the outlaw kept a low profile in the county because of his indictment for horse theft. As a result, only a few people sighted him around the time of the England murders. Douglass felt that if he dug a little deeper, however, he could prove that Bill Taylor passed through Red River Station on the day after the slayings. Red River Station, twenty miles north/northwest of the England home, was a small hamlet in north central Montague County established in 1860 just south of the Red River on Salt Creek.[6]

Douglass's remark about Bill Taylor being at Red River Station harkens back to Ben Krebs's second trial in February 1879 at Gainesville. During that trial, Krebs's attorneys had filed a motion for a continuance in order that three men might have time to travel to Cooke County and testify about Bill Taylor's whereabouts during the time of the England murders. District Judge J. A. Carroll denied the continuance and the jury never heard the testimony of Joseph and Wilborn Cothrum and John Walker. Walker was to have testified that "early in the morning after the murder of the England family, Bill Taylor, accompanied by one Charles Hall and another person, passed his (Walker's) house, and informed him of the murder, exhibiting a bright-barrelled [sic] six-shooter which he said was at the shooting." For their part, the Cothrums would have testified "to the same effect, with the addition that Bill Taylor said that he was at the murder and fired the pistol and that Hall and another person assisted in the slaughter."[7]

Piecing together these various threads, Douglass and others now believed that the guilty parties in the England murders were not Ben Krebs, James Preston, and Aaron Taylor, but John Music, Bill Taylor, and Charles Hall. John Music held a personal grudge against the Englands, especially against the vindictive and spiteful Selena. Even though Selena had legally purchased the Savage Survey, John Music had formed the conclusion (however illogical) that the Englands were illegally squatting on property that rightfully belonged to his father. Music and Bill Taylor were out hunting on the day of the England murders and likely hatched the plan for the nighttime attack during their hunt. Music may have told Taylor that the Englands had plenty of money and had just built a fine new home. Robbery and murder were nothing new for Bill Taylor. By this point in his life, he had killed his own father and joined a gang of outlaws, committing crimes on both sides of the Red River. In an effort to burnish his reputation as a desperado, Taylor openly bragged about his involvement in the England murders and proudly displayed his revolver to several people. Charles Hall was a criminal associate of Taylor's and likely part of the same gang.

Another statement Elbridge Douglass secured during his investigation was from Louis Fred Fisch, a native of Switzerland and a well-respected resident of Montague County since 1867. Fisch's affidavit, like Luna Dickerson's, contained several major revelations. Fisch said it was paramount that several examples of the "old prejudice or as I may term it, rascality of old, may be brought to light." Vital evidence was suppressed during the trials and a number of individuals, fearful of violent retribution, refused to testify because "of the excited and prejudiced feeling then existing . . . [among] county officials and other citizens of this county against said Krebs and Preston."[8]

Fisch next leveled a serious accusation against Montague County Attorney Avery Lenoir Matlock. He said that when Matlock and Sheriff Lee Perkins arrested Krebs, Preston, and Taylor, Fisch thought the trio was innocent. He offered to help Matlock prove this. If Matlock would jail Fisch on some charge, he would gain Krebs's confidence and learn the full story. Fisch stated, "My services were contemptuously refused by Hon. A. L. Matlock with the reply, 'Fisch we've got the party we want and don't want any others and if you speak in favor or in any way try to get them clear, I will get the Vigilantes (then operating in our county) to attend to you.' *A fine county attorney and a very fine champion of democracy!*" (emphasis in original). Here, then, is the county attorney, sworn to uphold the laws of Texas, allegedly admitting to Fisch that he actively cooperated with a group of vigilantes in Montague County and threatening to have Fisch lynched by these vigilantes if he interfered.[9]

Fisch had more to say regarding Matlock's conduct. He heard several people tell the county attorney that Bill Taylor was seen skulking near the England home the day after the murders and that Taylor was a fugitive from Montague County wanted for horse theft. Despite this information, Matlock and Perkins made no attempt to find him. In addition, Bill Taylor's sister, Rhoda Krebs, and her husband, Ben, told Fisch that Bill had been at their home the day preceding the slayings. Fisch had been afraid to tell the sheriff about Taylor's whereabouts himself because "I knew full well the desperate character of Taylor" and his outlaw accomplices. Since Fisch was not an officer of the county, he could not legally carry a weapon with which to defend himself.[10]

Concluding his affidavit to Governor Hogg, Fisch said, "I will state again that the feeling in this county against . . . Krebs and Preston was vindictive and bitter without cause and that it was very unsafe for a person to utter one word in favor or about . . . Krebs and Preston, as in fact at those times our county was infested with cutthroats on one hand and vigilantes on the other and intimidating, unscrupulous officers of the peace between, so that the timid and law-abiding citizen had to take the background." Considering these circumstances, it was inevitable that Krebs, Preston, and Taylor were convicted. They never stood a chance of receiving fair and impartial trials.[11]

The last affidavit Elbridge Douglass secured during his October 1894 trip to Montague was from James M. Grigsby, brother of William H. Grigsby, who helped defend Krebs, Preston, and Aaron Taylor. James Grigsby later served as Ochiltree

County judge from 1921 to 1930, and Ochiltree County justice of the peace from 1931 until his death in 1936. Grigsby stated that he had known Ben Krebs for many years prior to the murders and that area residents had always considered him to be of good character and repute. Grigsby noted that "when he was accused of said murder many of the old residents were astounded and did not believe the charges, as Mr. Krebs had led such an exemplary life amongst them through all the Indian Troubles." Grigsby said that J. A. Carroll, the presiding judge for all of the England trials, had told him that the trustworthiness of one witness was suspect and that his letter to Governor Roberts asking for the commutations "was one of the proudest actions of his life." Grigsby believed that pardoning "these two poor old men" would be strongly supported by most Montague County residents.[12]

Regarding Selena England and her deathbed identification of Ben Krebs, Grigsby noted that her credibility as a witness was questionable. "Mr. James Doke, her neighbor [at Whitesboro] in Grayson County, told me he would not take her testimony," he said, "[and] that if she was prejudiced against anyone she would swear falsely if she knew death was immediate." Doke's comment to Grigsby corroborated other statements made throughout the years regarding Selena England's character and the veracity of her dying declarations.[13]

Several weeks after receiving Elbridge Douglass's investigative report, and with the year 1894 and his tenure as governor both rapidly drawing to a close, James Stephen Hogg did something that previous Texas governors Roberts, Ireland, and Ross had refused to do. On November 28, 1894, the day before Thanksgiving, he pardoned Ben Krebs and James Preston. In prefacing his reasons for the pardons, Hogg noted, "Of all the cases that I have ever read or that have appeared before me for consideration, this is the strangest, most novel and peculiar. . . . The blackest pages of criminal justice do not portray or present a blacker or more fiendish deed than the destruction of the England family."[14]

Regarding his reasoning, Governor Hogg related that it was James Preston's personal letter to him in November 1891 that sparked his conscience and compelled him to take action. After thoroughly studying Preston's pardon file, Hogg reached the conclusion that the Rusk inmate was innocent. In listing the key factors that influenced his decision, the governor noted the statement from Rusk Penitentiary Assistant Superintendent J. P. Gibson that more than ninety officers, guards, and employees in the prison believed in Krebs's and Preston's innocence. In addition, according to attorney Lucas Smith and Texas Court of Criminal Appeals Chief Justice J. M. Hurt, both of whom served as defense lawyers during the trials, Harvey Taylor had sworn to them before God that Krebs and Preston were not involved in the England killings. Harvey had not stated so in his testimony because he was terrified that Montague County vigilantes would murder him. Hogg believed that the crux of the matter was misidentification. Harvey, being two feet away from and face-to-face with one of the killers, was more likely to correctly identify the man than his mother, whose back was to the same man while he chased her and her daughter in the yard. Selena said she recognized Krebs by his beard and hat, but Harvey was positive the murderer wore no hat and had only a mustache.[15]

The governor next turned to Luna Dickerson, former wife of John Music, who had stated under oath that Harvey Taylor told Selena England, in Luna's presence, that one of the killers was Bill Taylor and another was John Music. Then there was Aaron Taylor who, when on his deathbed in Huntsville, asserted to Col. T. J. Goree, superintendent of the Texas Prison system, that he, Krebs, and Preston had had nothing to do with the England murders. Goree believed him. Finally, L. D. Brooks and F. R. Lubbock of the Texas Board of Pardon Advisers had studied the case in depth, reported to Hogg that they believed Krebs and Preston were suffering punishment for the misdeeds of others, and recommended both men be pardoned immediately.[16]

In his detailed analysis of the case, Hogg next addressed the issue of motive. Who had a motive to kill the Englands? Hogg said that whoever committed the deed deserved the death penalty. The question was, Who were the guilty parties? "It is true that the Krebs and England family were on unfriendly terms as neighbors" and that the Englands had filed a misdemeanor assault complaint against Krebs, which was pending trial at the time of the murders. Hogg pointed out, however, "So it may be noted that John Musick [sic], another neighbor, was also 'at outs' with the England family because, he claimed, they had taken the land they occupied from his father, and thus had deprived himself of valuable property rights."[17]

Regarding James Preston, the governor observed that Preston and the Englands "were good friends, so much so that but a few months before the homicide Mr. England had preached the funeral of Preston's deceased wife." So, even though Krebs was furious at the Englands, Preston was not. "If Krebs was their enemy, Preston was their friend. If Krebs had a motive, Preston had not." Turning to John Music's motivations, Hogg noted that if one focused on other aspects of the case, "it may be said that if Krebs was unfriendly to the Englands, so was Mr. Music, their other neighbor. If Krebs had malice towards them, so had Music. If Krebs had a motive, Music had one quite as strong." Hogg pointed to other incriminating evidence: John Music and Bill Taylor had been out hunting together on the evening of the murders, Music had been "unfriendly to the Englands about the land claim, [Bill] Taylor had not been seen in the neighborhood since [the murders, and] soon after, . . . Music wound up his affairs, quit his wife and family and left the country and has not returned. Additional to this, his conduct and insinuations about the tragedy more or less cast suspicion on him."[18]

Hogg closed his pardon statement with the assurance that he had "taken the time commensurate with the grave responsibility resting upon me and have carefully examined into the whole case. My deliberate opinion, formed without bias, fear or favor, is that both Krebs and Preston are innocent men. May the Great God, the keeper of my conscience and soul, decide that I am right. Ben Krebs and James Preston are fully pardoned to all their rights and citizenship." Governor Hogg followed the time-honored tradition of many politicians before and since, who issued pardons near the end of their terms. During his time in office, Hogg commuted ten death sentences for murder in the first degree to life in prison and pardoned ten life sentences for murder, exactly the same number as Governor Roberts. Although Hogg took several years to make his decision, his conscience and fortitude ensured that Krebs and Preston, unlike Aaron Taylor, did not die in prison.[19]

Governor Hogg's pardons generated considerable backlash, showing that almost twenty years later, the England murder case still engendered strong feelings among both the press and the public. One reader of the *Galveston Daily News*, M. M. Kenney, wrote a letter to the editor stating that in the interest of full and truthful public disclosure, elements of Hogg's pardon statement deserved criticism. Kenney was upset that the governor had disparaged circumstantial evidence that the investigators had uncovered. In Kenney's opinion, such proof was the best kind available to prosecutors. He asserted that Krebs and Preston were each convicted by two juries, juries that judged the circumstantial evidence as conclusive.[1]

Kenney pointed out that the governor's rationale for the pardons did not address key facts in the case, such as Krebs's bloody shirt and the three sets of footprints leading toward the Krebs home. He also did not believe Harvey Taylor's identification of Bill Taylor and John Music and was contemptuous of the theory that these men killed the England family. Kenney retorted, "If the best evidence that can be offered to human reason is to be set aside for such twaddle . . . it is time to tear down the courthouses and appeal to the laws of nature, which are not written but which cannot be repealed." Here, as late as 1894, the implied threat resurfaces that if Texas's judicial system could not handle its criminals, vigilante mobs would.[2]

Kenney's reference to the laws of nature evoked painful memories of lynchings and Indian raids, memories that were still fresh in residents' minds at the end of the nineteenth century. The years of terrifying violence and turbulence during North Texas's frontier period had traumatized citizens. Discussing the controversy provoked by Hogg's pardons, the *Gainesville Daily Hesperian* reminded its readers of the England murders' impact upon North Texans in 1876. "Our people were wrought up to the highest pitch," and Governor Roberts's commutation of Krebs's and Preston's death sentences in April 1880 "raised a perfect storm against him here." The newspaper noted, "There came near being a mob at Gainesville over the affair on the day [L. M.] Noffsinger [*sic*] was hanged. The people in their anger, loudly threatened to release Noffsinger, not because he was innocent, but because Krebs and Preston were not hanged too."[3]

The *Hesperian* also detailed the heartbreaking repercussions of the England case on Krebs, Preston, and their families. For decades, Krebs had been a well-respected citizen with a good reputation. After his arrest and imprisonment in the fall of 1876, his friends and circle of support evaporated. Preston confronted similar ostracism. Commenting on the regional hysteria engendered by the killings, the reporter pointed out that while there were some, "cool headed and careful, who contended that the men were being made to suffer for the crime of another . . . their voices were drowned out in the general clamor for blood."[4]

Whereas the *Hesperian* article was generally approving of Hogg's actions, the *Galveston Daily News* offered its readers a more ambivalent response, including a scathing critique of Texas's legal system. A *News* reporter opined that Governors Roberts and Hogg had made a mess of the England murder case. As a result, the state's criminal justice system had lost considerable credibility with citizens. "The crime for which these two men were convicted was one of the most diabolical ever committed in Texas," and if Krebs and Preston were guilty, "their necks should have been broken" years ago. If, however, they were innocent, Roberts should have granted them a full pardon in 1880, rather than leaving them to suffer fourteen years at hard labor in Texas's abominable prison system.[5]

For the reporter, the choice was one or the other, there was no middle ground. But the *News* was engaging in black-or-white thinking formulated with the benefit of hindsight. Throughout, the England case had never been clear-cut, making an informed decision difficult. Key evidence came to light in pieces over two decades. Without the full picture, the potential for error was high. Men's lives were at stake. Neither governor wanted innocent blood on his hands, but at the same time, neither wanted to mistakenly set at liberty two merciless murderers. Nevertheless, the reporter insisted that "a terrible blunder" had occurred: "The men have either been outraged or justice in Texas has been outraged by two governors, and it is now a foregone conclusion that the cold-blooded murder of the Englands eighteen years ago will be forever unavenged." The *News* article complained about the unnecessary delays, the lack of speedy justice in the legal system, and the uneven application of justice. Taking almost twenty years to pardon two blameless men who had no money or influence was unconscionable given that guilty criminals routinely escaped justice thanks to their wealth and friends in high places.[6]

One prominent thread in the newspaper commentary that followed the governor's pardons was the issue of compensation. The *San Antonio Express* editorialized that Governor Hogg had taken the right course in pardoning Krebs and Preston, but that the pardons alone were not enough. The State of Texas should recompense the two men for all of their legal expenses, expenses which had left both families nearly destitute. Krebs and Preston should also be compensated for their mental and physical anguish and their many years of wrongful imprisonment at hard labor. The issue of compensation has long been controversial in Texas, and the debate continues to the present. The *Dallas Morning News* recently reported that prior to 2001, just two individuals had received financial recompense; each received $25,000. After 2001, increased use of DNA testing forced the State of Texas to re-examine its policies regarding wrongful imprisonment. Exonerees initially received $25,000 per year of incarceration or a $500,000 lump sum for twenty years or longer. The state later revised this to $50,000 per year, and $100,000 per year for inmates on death row.[7]

Several years later, Texas further adjusted its compensation policies in response to complaints regarding penniless exonerees who had exhausted their resources in legal fees. In 2009, the Texas legislature amended the law to entitle those who had been wrongly incarcerated to up to $80,000 for every year spent in prison, payable in one lump sum upon release. As of October 2017, the state had spent more than $109 million compensating exonerees. Back in 1894, for men like Krebs and Preston who had sold their all of their land and spent their life savings paying lawyers, there was no system of recompense.[8]

Appealing to readers' consciences, the *San Antonio Express* said that no financial amends could ever compensate for the severe deprivations Krebs and Preston had endured. Nonetheless, the State of Texas, "in fair honor and justice," should do all within its power to make the time remaining to the men as comfortable as possible. "These tottering old men, whose lives, fortunes, and characters have been so rudely wrecked, have claims against the state that cannot in honor be ignored." The *Waco News* fully agreed, arguing that Texas should recompense Krebs and Preston liberally. While money could not eradicate the wrongs of the past, the jingling of gold coins was still "a very comfortable sound in the pockets of aged men." The *Waco News* said that the state "cannot afford to appropriate itself the best portion of men's lives and then turn them out in their old age, perhaps homeless and helpless, to die in some obscure poorhouse."[9]

Responding to both the *San Antonio Express* and the *Waco News* commentaries on compensation, the *Galveston Daily News* editors were not swayed. Despite Hogg's pardons, a number of people were not convinced of Krebs's and Preston's innocence. Perhaps the men were blameless, but the cloud of guilt hanging over them had not entirely dispersed. The newspaper then raised a larger issue: if the two men were entitled to compensation, what about all the other persons equally deserving? "If these men are entitled to pay for the property, time, and happiness which the state robbed them of why not pay every innocent prisoner or citizen who is the victim of justice denied or justice delayed? Many innocent men lie in jail or walk anxiously under a blighting cloud of criminal accusation for years because of the indolence of public officials. . . . The state is very much in debt when one comes to figure up the score fairly."[10]

The *Galveston Daily News* pointed out that if Texas tried to recompense all entitled parties, the state treasury would soon be depleted. In contrast, the *Austin Statesman* strongly disagreed with this rationale, calling it "specious" and "untenable." The *Statesman* noted that in 1876 Krebs and Preston had been relatively young and of good repute, with close, loving families, "and in a moment their lives were changed to sorrows, their happy lives to woe unutterable, the hopes that clustered about their homes dashed from their lips and they were made to drink the bitter cup of humiliation and degradation to the dregs."[11]

The Austin paper reminded readers that Krebs and Preston were wrongly accused, and "in a moment of local excitement . . . [were] torn from the arms of wives and children and cast into prison, stripped of the garments of honorable citizens and clothed in the stripes of the prison." They were "compelled to work day after day, not for their families but for the state, and at night in a lonely cell to bedew their hard pillows with the unavailing tears of the innocent. Great God! Was there ever a greater wrong demanding a greater compensation, and to this appeal for some kind of compensation the miserable plea of the poverty of the state is made [by the *Galveston Daily News*]."[12]

In the end, the *News* proved right. Krebs and Preston received no compensation from the State of Texas for their personal and financial hardships. Providing a poignant close to its coverage of the England murder case, the *News* had a reporter on hand at the Ardmore, Indian Territory, station in early December 1894, when Ben Krebs stepped off the train. "An affecting scene was witnessed at the depot this afternoon shortly after the north bound passenger train steamed into the station. An old man, with shoulders bent and hair white from age, was met at the train by his two sons, whom he had not seen for more than 25 years. The old man was none other than Krebs, who was pardoned a few days ago by Governor Hogg after serving 18 years in the penitentiary."[13]

Ben Krebs moved into the family home at Lone Grove, Indian Territory, not far from present-day Ardmore, Oklahoma. In 1900, the Krebs household at Lone Grove consisted of Ben and his wife, Rhoda, son William, daughter Georgia Ann "Annie" and her husband, Napoleon D. "Poley" Davidson. James Preston also moved to Indian Territory upon his release from the Rusk Penitentiary. In 1900, Preston lived eighty miles northeast of Krebs, in Township 1, between present-day Tupelo and Clarita, Oklahoma. Also living in the Preston home were daughter Julia, son "Jimmy" James Jr., Jimmy's wife, Vesta, and their two children, Dallie and Rubie.[14]

James Preston lived for five and a half years after his release from prison, dying at age seventy-seven on June 27, 1900, at Lehigh, near Colgate, Oklahoma. Ben Krebs died eight months later, at age seventy-two, on February 21, 1901, at Newport, near Ardmore. In another twist of fate in a story replete with surprises, in 1928, James Preston's granddaughter, Winifred "Winnie" Preston, married Ben Krebs's son, William Benjamin Krebs. The descendants of the two men, forever linked by the England family murders, are now also connected by marriage. Winnie and William's son, William Preston "Little Bill" Krebs (born 1929), is the grandson of Ben Krebs and the great-grandson of James Preston. In 1930, Winnie, William, and ten-month-old Little Bill Krebs were living in Tulsa, Oklahoma, along with Winnie's parents, Elizabeth and John Warren Preston, James Preston's son.[15]

Little Bill says that his father never talked about the England family murders. For much of his life, he did not know what happened to his grandfather Ben Krebs and his great-grandfather James Preston. Little Bill remembers a story he later heard about his grandfather, John Warren Preston, James's son. One day while John was working on the railroad in Kansas, some of his fellow laborers started talking about Krebs, Preston, and the England case. "This came up, and some guy up there was mouthing off, you know, 'Hey, they ought to lynch those dirty so and sos,' and old John said, 'shut up, you don't know nothing what you're talking about.' And the guy just kept mouthing off, the legend is that he took a pick handle and laid him out and left the place and never did know if he had killed him or not."[16]

Little Bill also recalls two trips through the western and eastern United States that he and his parents took in 1939 and 1940, when he was ten and eleven. Whenever they would stop during these vacations, his father William would "wander off, you know, and go find some old boy . . . and ask him if he ever knew of a guy named Music. I figured he was just looking for some friend of his that he'd lost." William Krebs never located John R. Music. After deserting his wife, Luna, and their children in Wise County, Texas, Music returned to Arkansas. In June 1880, the thirty-one-year-old, illiterate farmhand was living at Richland (near present-day Wesley) in Madison County with his widowed mother, Louisa Perkins Music Gibson.[17]

By the early 1880s, John Music had moved again, this time 120 miles south to Scott County, Arkansas. In August 1883, John married for the third time, to thirty-three-year-old Charity E. Ramsey. Charity, a Georgia native, lived in Brawley, Arkansas, eleven miles west of Waldron. She died several years after their marriage and the couple had no children. From 1886 to 1888, John Music served as District 1 Road Overseer for Brawley Township. Music's district encompassed the southeastern corner of the township, along Jones Creek Road. By law, all persons living along thoroughfares were required to help maintain them.[18]

In July 1888, John Music married a fourth time, to fifty-two-year-old Olive Octavo Crandell Yancey (thirteen years his senior), in Brawley, Arkansas. Interestingly, Olive was also from Georgia and had been Charity Ramsey's neighbor in Brawley in 1880. Seven months after their marriage in February 1889, a Scott County man named Flood Rawlings sued John Music, claiming that Music had taken possession of land that he owned. Rawlings asserted that he held title to the acreage and wanted Music off his property, along with $200 in damages. Music eventually won the case in 1890 and Rawlings was ordered to pay all legal fees. John R. Music lived out his remaining years in obscurity on Jones Creek Road in Brawley under the shadow of the picturesque 1,582-foot Walker Mountain, part of the Ouachita Mountain range. In the 1900 census, Olive O. Musick [sic] was listed as a sixty-five-year-old widow living in Brawley, Arkansas, so John Music must have died in Scott County sometime before 1900.[19]

William Krebs was more successful in finding his uncle Bill Taylor, brother of Rhoda Krebs and Aaron Taylor. Little Bill recalls a story told to him by Vernon Williams, of Tulsa, Oklahoma. Sometime in 1933 or 1934, William Krebs asked

Vernon to drive him from Tulsa to Vinita, Oklahoma, sixty-five miles to the northeast. "Dad was never really able to drive to where he could get a license," according to Little Bill. "He was a horse and buggy guy, so anytime he could find somebody that had a little spare time, he'd get them to drive him places. So that's the reason this fellow named Vernon Williams was the driver. But anyway, Vernon drove him up there to Vinita. This guy [Bill Taylor] lived on the south edge of Vinita; it was out in the country."[20]

Vernon parked the car by the Taylor property, and he and William Krebs sat watching the house. Finally, when Bill Taylor stepped outside to do some chores, Krebs got out of the car. When "the old man came out to feed the hogs, . . . Dad maneuvered himself around between the old guy and the house, so that he couldn't get back there if he wanted to [get a weapon and] fight. What transpired we'll never know because he told Vernon to sit in the car. So, anyway, they talked for a while, there was no war or anything, and it broke up at that point; nobody did nothing, and they went home. And that was the first time he saw . . . [Bill Taylor]. Then, apparently, after that they saw each other fairly often and on a peaceful basis. And he got to know all of the Taylor relatives, and they were always friends, they always visited in their house." Little Bill later met several of the Taylor children. He says that his father "never blamed the offspring for what the old man did."[21]

For half a century, Bill Taylor concealed his whereabouts. After locals in Montague County spotted him crossing the Red River into Indian Territory the day after the England murders in 1876, he disappeared. He finally surfaced again in late 1924, when he filed a pension application with the Veterans Administration for his three months' service in the Texas Rangers during 1873–74. The seventy-one-year-old Taylor told the Veterans Administration that he had been a farmer but was now disabled and could not work, so he needed money. Taylor's pension application shines a light on his activities during the missing years from 1876 to 1924. After leaving Texas, he passed through Indian Territory en route to his home state of Missouri. In late summer 1876, he showed up on foot at the Benton County, Missouri, farm belonging to his brother, Robert Hampton Taylor.[22]

Living next door to Robert were the Franklin family, which included fourteen-year-old Julia Franklin. A relationship blossomed between the twenty-three-year-old Bill Taylor and young Julia, and the two were wed just over the county line, in Morgan County, Missouri, on March 27, 1877, by Rev. Richard Brady. Bill and Julia were together only a short time. In April or early May 1877, Taylor abandoned his now-pregnant bride without warning. Taylor later claimed he left her because she was married to another man. While it is true that Julia was separated but not yet legally divorced from her first husband, the real reason Bill Taylor left her was because he had stolen another horse. Locals in Benton County—including Robert Taylor, Julia, and her brother Hiram Franklin—recalled that Bill got drunk and stole a horse from a farmer named Joe Allen. It was not long before local law enforcement officials came looking for Bill, who abruptly abandoned the horse and fled south to Indian Territory. By year's end, Julia had given birth to a daughter she named Lizzie. Bill Taylor later claimed that he and Julia had no children together, but the evidence shows otherwise.[23]

After fleeing Missouri in the spring of 1877, Bill Taylor settled in Indian Territory. On March 15, 1878, he married twenty-year-old Nancy Matilda Lucas at Oaks Mission. Nancy and Bill eventually moved to the outskirts of Vinita, Oklahoma, where they had thirteen children and worked a small farm on the south side of town. When the couple became elderly and Bill was no longer able to work, they moved into Vinita.[24]

In 1925, T. Quinn Jones, special inspector examiner for the Bureau of Pensions, interviewed Bill Taylor at Vinita to verify the information in Taylor's pension application. In reviewing Taylor's Texas Ranger service, the government found that someone had signed his name to his Ranger company's muster roll. Taylor insisted that it was not him because he was illiterate and could not sign his name. The discrepancy led the Pension Bureau to launch an investigation. In his interview with Special Inspector Jones, Taylor stated that he was born in Missouri on August 22, 1853, he grew up in Montague County, Texas, and his parents were William Taylor and Jane Taylor. Among his siblings he listed Eliza "Rhoda" Taylor and Aaron K. Taylor. During Jones's background checks on Taylor in Missouri, several locals had mentioned that Bill might have killed his father in Texas, but Jones did not pursue the matter. Neither did the inspector visit Montague County, where he would have learned that residents suspected Bill of participating in the England family murders.[25]

After concluding his investigation of Bill Taylor's pension application, Jones told his superiors that Taylor "seems to be an honest old fellow and appreciative, but very ignorant." Locals in Vinita informed Jones that Taylor previously had a reputation for drinking "up his money as fast as he could," but that in recent years he had "quit his drinking habits." Ultimately, in May 1926, the government approved Bill Taylor's Indian Wars Pension and issued him a check for $2,180, along with a pension of $30 per month, which increased to $50 per month by 1934.[26]

Bill Taylor died of pneumonia in Vinita, Oklahoma, on September 10, 1934. When he passed, he left no money and no property to his widow, Nancy, who lacked the funds to pay for his funeral and a headstone. Nancy Taylor applied to the Veterans Administration for help. Detailing her financial straits, she told the federal government that she had not paid taxes in 1933 or in any other year because she had never had an income to pay taxes on. Eventually, the Veterans Administration approved funds for a headstone and paid $100 of Taylor's $233.50 funeral costs. The family buried William Barnett "Bill" Taylor at Fairview Cemetery in Vinita, Oklahoma.[27]

It has been almost a century and a half since William England, Selena England, and two of her children, Susie and Isaiah Taylor, were murdered six miles south of Montague, Texas. Today, the Krebs, England, and Music homes are long gone. All that remains are foundation stones; bits of glass, china, and crockery; and, at the England residence, a rock-lined well. As to who the guilty parties in the England family murders were, we are left with a wide divergence of opinion. Some like Finis Piner, who prosecuted the case, were immovable in their declarations of Ben Krebs's, James Preston's, and Aaron Taylor's guilt. Others were just as strongly persuaded of their innocence, and pointed to John Music, Bill Taylor, and Charles Hall as the likely perpetrators. A third group, including Governors Roberts and Hogg, largely believed Krebs, Preston, and Taylor to be innocent, but were never completely sure.[28]

While some doubts linger, one thing is certain. No matter one's perspective on the England murder case, it was both a human tragedy and a miscarriage of justice. The legal aftermath involved five Texas governors, five trials at Montague and Gainesville, and five appeals to the Texas Court of Appeals. For anyone interested in Texas and its legal history, the case offers a realistic snapshot of frontier justice and retribution in North Texas following the Civil War.

When asked about his grandfather Ben Krebs, great-grandfather James Preston, and the question of whether the State of Texas owed their families anything, Little Bill Krebs replied, "Oh, I don't know where you can make restitution for doing anything like that or not. I think what they needed [was] that all the lawyers that railroaded them ought to have been disbarred, [that] would have been more restitution as far as I'm concerned. . . . Well, I don't think about it too much because I don't like the feelings. . . . I don't know, there's no point now, it's too late for everything. They let them out of the place [prison] at least, [it] probably took the right guy in office [Hogg], and the fact that everything had cooled down, [and] they were old. The Krebs are all gone [now] because I don't have any male children. So that's the end of the Krebs business."[29]

NOTES

Chapter 1

1. "*A. K. Taylor v. The State*, 1877," in A. M. Jackson and A. M. Jackson Jr., *Cases Argued and Adjudged in the Court of Appeals of the State of Texas* (St. Louis, MO: Gilbert Book Co., 1878), 3:170–71. Although the witnesses and evidence presented here are from Aaron K. Taylor's June 1877 trial, the testimony and evidence in Ben Krebs's November 1876 trial were virtually identical. See also 1870 U.S. Federal Census, Grayson County, Texas, M593, R1588, 52, National Archives and Records Administration (hereafter NA). The moon phase on August 26, 1876, from NASA, "Moon Phases: 1801–1900," http://eclipse.gsfc.nasa.gov/phase/phases1801.html (accessed April 15, 2013), and from U.S. Naval Observatory, "Moon Phases," http://tycho.usno.navy.mil/cgi-bin/vphase -post.sh (accessed April 15, 2013). The new moon occurred on August 19, 1876, and the full moon on September 3, 1876. Isaiah Taylor's wedding was set for August 29, 1876. See *Galveston Daily News*, February 15, 1880.
2. "*A. K. Taylor v. The State*, 1877," in Jackson and Jackson, *Cases Argued and Adjudged in the Court of Appeals*, 3:171.
3. "*A. K. Taylor v. The State*, 1877," 171. Artist Gary Zaboly made a nighttime drawing of the England crime scene for the author, entitled "The Uninvited."
4. "*A. K. Taylor v. The State*, 1877," 171 (quotation 1), 172 (quotation 2).
5. "*A. K. Taylor v. The State*, 1877," 174.
6. "*A. K. Taylor v. The State*, 1877," 174.
7. "*A. K. Taylor v. The State*, 1877," 174.
8. "*A. K. Taylor v. The State*, 1877," 173.
9. "*A. K. Taylor v. The State*, 1877," 173 (quotations 1, 2, and 4), 175 (quotation 3).

10. "*A. K. Taylor v. The State, 1877,*" 172.

11. "*A. K. Taylor v. The State, 1877,*" 172, 173 (quotations).

12. "*A. K. Taylor v. The State, 1877,*" 172.

13. "*A. K. Taylor v. The State, 1877,*" 175–76. Regarding possible meanings of "Dutchman," see chap. 3, note 1.

14. "*A. K. Taylor v. The State, 1877,*" 175. James Preston was born on February 28, 1823, the son of George and Anna Preston. On March 4, 1847, he married Martha Elizabeth Rice at the Church of Christ on the Middle Fork of the Grand River, in Van Buren County, Missouri. During their twenty-nine-year marriage, James and Martha (born in Tennessee on April 30, 1828) had ten children. On December 10, 1872, James Preston purchased 242 acres in the McKinney & Williams Survey, Abstract 508, which bordered the William H. Taylor Survey to the east, and the Wiley B. Savage (Krebs property) and Thomas N. Savage Surveys (England property) to the south. During 1873, Preston also purchased shares in the William H. Taylor and Wiley B. Savage Surveys. Martha Preston died in February 1876, near Bowie, TX. James Preston biographical information from Joyce E. Whatley Family Genealogy Research Book (given to the author by Whatley's daughter Cheryl Rivera). Whatley was a relative who received much of her information directly from James Preston's granddaughter Winifred Preston (born November 28, 1900 in Bowie, TX). Winifred was the daughter of James Preston's son John Warren Preston. See also "James Preston Family Tree," Ancestry.com, https://www.ancestry.com/family-tree/person/tree/32942697/person/29338469893/facts (accessed December 4, 2018); McKinney & Williams Survey, Montague County, TX, Abstract 508, Texas General Land Office Archives (hereafter GLO); Montague County Deed Record Book A, May 10, 1873, 318, and July 14, 1873, 649, and August 30, 1873, 718; Montague County Deed Record Book B, November 10, 1873, 154–55; 1850 U.S. Federal Census, Cass County, MO, M432, R395, 110B, NA; 1860 U.S. Federal Census, Cass County, MO, M653, R612, 798, NA; 1870 U.S. Federal Census, Jasper County, MO, M593, R783, 5A, NA; "Missouri, Compiled Marriages, 1754–1850," Ancestry.com, 112–13 (accessed December 4, 2018).

15. "*A. K. Taylor v. The State, 1877,*" in Jackson and Jackson, *Cases Argued and Adjudged in the Court of Appeals,* 3:175–76.

16. "*A. K. Taylor v. The State, 1877,*" 176.

17. "*A. K. Taylor v. The State, 1877,*" 176. Regarding "Dutch talk," see chap. 3, note 1.

18. "*A. K. Taylor v. The State, 1877,*" 176; *Denison Daily News,* August 29, 1876 (quotations). I visited Ben Dye Cemetery near Whitesboro in January 2017. It is now an overgrown, dense thicket. Fortunately, local historian Ruth Varley conducted a detailed inventory of the cemetery before it fell into disuse. Varley later gave her Ben Dye inventory to Liz Hunt Reedy, who posted it online. The cemetery is named after Ben R. Dye (1845–1902). Eight other Dye family members are also buried there. The graves range in date from the 1870s to the 1940s. Varley's inventory lists four England graves marked with red rocks. During my 2017 inventory of the entire Ben Dye Cemetery, I found only four such graves. All had bright red sandstone markers. Liz Hunt Reedy, Whitesboro,

TX, telephone interview with the author, January 2017; "Ben Dye Cemetery, Grayson County," Cemeteries of Texas, http://www.usgennet.org/usa/tx/topic/cemeteries/Etx/ Grayson/cemetery/bendye.htm (accessed December 23, 2018).

In September 1876, two weeks after the murders, the surviving children of Selena Taylor England and Billington Taylor appointed their brother Joe Taylor to serve as the agent and administrator of Selena's and Susie Taylor's estates. The probate court also appointed Joe Taylor as administrator of William England's estate. See Montague County Court Minutes, Book No. 1, September 9, 1876, and November 20, 1876, 29–30, 35, 46. The surviving Taylor children, who likely had no desire to revisit the murder scene, abandoned the England homestead on the Thomas N. Savage Survey. County authorities seized the land for nonpayment of $3.72 in back taxes. John. H. Stephens subsequently purchased the 160-acre parcel in a June 1879 public auction for $9.72. See Montague County Deed Record Book H, June 3, 1879, 47–49.

Regarding the theory that the killers targeted the Englands for robbery because of their wealth, Grayson County tax rolls for 1873 show Selena England with a net worth of $2,195, including 3 horses, 16 head of cattle, 10 sheep, and 450 acres. William England had a net worth of $760, including 1 horse, 6 head of cattle, and 190 acres. Montague County tax rolls for 1876 show that Selena England, not her husband, was the owner of the Thomas N. Savage Survey. At that time Selena also had 1 horse, 30 cattle, and 30 goats and hogs for a net worth of $698. William England was not listed in the 1876 Montague County tax rolls. In sum, the Englands were not wealthy in comparison to their neighbors, including the Krebs, who in 1876 had a net worth of $675. See Montague County, TX, 1858–89 Tax Rolls, Reel 1, and Grayson County, TX, 1846–1878 Tax Rolls, Reel 1, Texas State Library and Archives Commission (hereafter TSLAC).

19. *Austin Weekly Democratic Statesman,* September 9, 1876.

20. *Galveston Daily News,* September 5, 1876.

21. "*A. K. Taylor v. The State,* 1877," in Jackson and Jackson, *Cases Argued and Adjudged in the Court of Appeals,* 3:188–89, 195–96, 200–201; "*Ben Krebs v. The State,* 1880," in Jackson and Jackson, *Cases Argued and Adjudged in the Court of Appeals of the State of Texas* (St. Louis: Gilbert Book Co., 1880), 8:19.

22. "*A. K. Taylor v. The State,* 1877," 176, 177.

23. "*A. K. Taylor v. The State,* 1877," 177–78.

24. "*A. K. Taylor v. The State,* 1877," 178. Regarding Montague County Attorney Matlock's failure to make cast impressions of the three sets of shoes at the England crime scene, Dwane Hilderbrand of the Scottsdale, AZ, Police Crime Laboratory says, "Footwear impression evidence examinations have been carried out and applied for forensic purposes for over 200 years. . . . The oldest recorded forensic footwear identification dates from . . . the autumn of 1786." See Dwane S. Hilderbrand, "Four Basic Components of Footwear Examination," Iowa Division of the International Association for Identification, http://www.iowaiai.org/four-basic-components-of-a-footwear-examination-2/ (accessed January 22, 2019). For an excellent overview of law enforcement and Texas's criminal justice system during this period see Bill Neal, *Getting Away with Murder*

on the Texas Frontier: Notorious Killings and Celebrated Trials (Lubbock: Texas Tech University Press, 2006), 5–24, 241–44.

25. "*A. K. Taylor v. The State*, 1877," 195–96, 200–201.

26. *Galveston Daily News*, October 6, 1876.

Chapter 2

1. Kenneth F. Neighbours, "Elm Creek Raid," *Handbook of Texas Online*, https:// tshaonline.org/handbook/online/articles/bte01 (accessed April 14, 2019); Allen Lee Hamilton, "Warren Wagontrain Raid," *Handbook of Texas Online*, https://tshaonline .org/handbook/online/articles/btw03 (accessed April 14, 2019); Glen Sample Ely, *The Texas Frontier and the Butterfield Overland Mail, 1858–1861* (Norman: University of Oklahoma Press, 2016), 92–93; Allen Lee Hamilton, *Sentinel of the Southern Plains: Fort Richardson and the Northwest Texas Frontier, 1866–1878* (Fort Worth: Texas Christian University Press, 1988), 147–51; Cliff D. Cates, *Pioneer History of Wise County* (St. Louis, MO: Nixon-Jones Printing, 1907), 168–70, 174–78, 215–17; Marvin F. London, *Indian Raids in Montague County* (St. Jo, TX: SJT Printers, 1977), 71–74, 81–83; A. Morton Smith, *The First 100 Years in Cooke County* (San Antonio, TX: Naylor Co., 1955), 46–49.

2. London, *Indian Raids in Montague County*, 71, 72 (quotation), 73.

3. Dorman H. Winfrey and James M. Day, eds., *The Indian Papers of Texas and the Southwest, 1825–1916* (Austin: Texas State Historical Association, 1995), 4:344–47.

4. Glen Sample Ely, *Where the West Begins: Debating Texas Identity* (Lubbock: Texas Tech University Press, 2011), 35–74; Glen Sample Ely, "Gone from Texas and Trading with the Enemy: New Perspectives on Civil War West Texas," in *Lone Star Blue and Gray: Essays on Texas and the Civil War*, 2nd ed., ed. Ralph A. Wooster and Robert Wooster (Denton: Texas State Historical Association, 2015), 161–84.

5. Ely, *Where the West Begins*, 50.

6. Ely, "Gone from Texas," 171.

7. "Frontier Battalion," *Handbook of Texas Online*, https://tshaonline.org/handbook /online/articles/qqf01 (accessed November 24, 2018).

8. Winfrey and Day, *Indian Papers of Texas*, 4:112 (quotations 1–3), 113. For ease of reading, I have cleaned up Whaley's letter to Throckmorton, correcting numerous spelling and grammatical errors.

9. Winfrey and Day, *Indian Papers of Texas*, 113.

10. Winfrey and Day, *Indian Papers of Texas*, 117.

11. Winfrey and Day, *Indian Papers of Texas*, 246 (quotations), 247. One of those signing the petition was Cash McDonald who, nine years later, would serve as the jury foreman during Ben Krebs's first trial for the England murders.

12. Winfrey and Day, *Indian Papers of Texas*, 148–52, 155–56, 211.

13. Hamilton, *Sentinel of the Southern Plains*, 15, 16 (quotation), 37; Loyd M. Uglow, *Standing in the Gap: Army Outposts, Picket Stations, and the Pacification of the Texas Frontier, 1866–1886* (Fort Worth: Texas Christian University Press, 2001), 88–95;

James L. Haley, "Red River War," *Handbook of Texas Online*, https://tshaonline.org/handbook/online/articles/qdr02 (accessed April 14, 2019).

14. Richard Maxwell Brown, *Strain of Violence: Historical Studies of American Violence and Vigilantism* (New York: Oxford University Press, 1975), 96, 101, 112.

15. Brown, *Strain of Violence*, 112 (quotation 1), 113 (quotation 2).

16. Ely, *Texas Frontier and the Butterfield Overland Mail*, 109.

17. Ely, *Texas Frontier and the Butterfield Overland Mail*, 106–9.

18. Ely, *Texas Frontier and the Butterfield Overland Mail*, 109.

19. Ely, *Texas Frontier and the Butterfield Overland Mail*, 105 (quotation 1), 106 (quotation 2), 111–12.

20. Ely, *Texas Frontier and the Butterfield Overland Mail*, 33.

21. Ely, *Texas Frontier and the Butterfield Overland Mail*, 33; Richard B. McCaslin, *Tainted Breeze: The Great Hanging at Gainesville, Texas, 1862* (Baton Rouge: Louisiana State University Press, 1994), 9–17.

22. Ely, *Texas Frontier and the Butterfield Overland Mail*, 35–36. Texans' anxieties reached a feverish pitch after October 16, 1859, when the radical abolitionist John Brown attacked the federal arsenal at Harpers Ferry, Virginia, intent on fomenting a violent slave insurrection. Proslavery residents of North Texas's Red River region were certain that John Brown types would soon infiltrate their communities and incite dissension. The match setting fire to the tinder was not long in coming. North Texas succumbed to a full-scale panic nine months later, after a series of fires broke out in Dallas, Denton, and Pilot Point in the summer of 1860. Convinced that persons of a John Brown mindset had set the fires to spark a slave revolt, local vigilante committees killed between thirty and one hundred people, both black and white. Law enforcement officials looked the other way as lawless brigands carried out their bloody work. Evidence later revealed that the conflagrations were accidental, caused by the "exceedingly hot summer" and local merchants' stocks of "new and volatile phosphorous matches." See Donald E. Reynolds, "Texas Troubles," in *Handbook of Texas Online*, https://tshaonline.org/handbook/online/articles/vetbr (accessed November 20, 2019).

23. Ely, *Texas Frontier and the Butterfield Overland Mail*, 36.

24. Ely, *Texas Frontier and the Butterfield Overland Mail*, 36 (quotation); McCaslin, *Tainted Breeze*, 60–83, 145; Smith, *First 100 Years in Cooke County*, 34–38; Pike County Archives and History Society, "Abner M. Hancock," *The Gems of Pike County, Arkansas* 8, no. 1 (Winter 1997), 14–16, http://www.pcahs.org/gems/GEMSV8N1.pdf (accessed November 5, 2019).

25. Ely, *Texas Frontier and the Butterfield Overland Mail*, 37 (quotations); Thomas Barrett, *The Great Hanging at Gainesville, Cooke County, Texas, October A.D. 1862* (Austin: Texas State Historical Association, 1961), 7.

26. Barry A. Crouch and Donaly E. Brice, *The Governor's Hounds: The Texas State Police, 1870–1873* (Austin: University of Texas Press, 2011), 19 (quotation), 20.

27. Cates, *Pioneer History of Wise County*, 150–53; McCaslin, *Tainted Breeze*, 160, 162 (quotation), 163–72; Winfrey and Day, *Indian Papers of Texas*, 216.

28. Winfrey and Day, *Indian Papers of Texas,* 216.

29. Winfrey and Day, *Indian Papers of Texas,* 216 (quotation 1), 217 (quotation 2).

30. Winfrey and Day, *Indian Papers of Texas,* 217 (quotations); Brett J. Derbes, "William Thomas Green Weaver," in *Handbook of Texas Online,* https://tshaonline.org/handbook/online/articles/fwe90 (accessed April 17, 2019). Five months after Weaver filed this report, Union commanders removed him as district judge of the Seventh Judicial District and replaced him with Hardin Hart. Weaver died in 1876 at his home in Gainesville from an overdose of chloral hydrate, a hypnotic sedative.

31. William L. Richter, *The Army in Texas during Reconstruction, 1865–1870* (College Station: Texas A&M University Press, 1987), 148.

32. Robert K. DeArment, *Bravo of the Brazos: John Larn of Fort Griffin, Texas* (Norman: University of Oklahoma Press, 2002), 54 (quotations), 66, 82–83, 107, 134–36; Ty Cashion, *A Texas Frontier: The Clear Fork Country and Fort Griffin, 1849–1887* (Norman: University of Oklahoma Press, 1996), 213–231.

33. "The Brown Brothers," *Galveston Daily News,* November 22, 1879.

34. *Galveston Daily News,* November 22, 1879.

35. *Galveston Daily News,* November 22, 1879.

36. *Galveston Daily News,* November 22, 1879.

37. *Galveston Daily News,* November 22, 1879.

38. DeArment, *Bravo of the Brazos,* 73 (quotation 1), 76–77 (quotation 2).

39. William D. Carrigan, *The Making of Lynching Culture: Violence and Vigilantism in Central Texas, 1836–1916* (Urbana: University of Illinois Press, 2004), 107.

40. Michael Ariens, email to the author, September 11, 2019 (quotation 1); Ariens, interview with the author, San Antonio, TX, August 20, 2015 (quotation 2); Wayne Gard, *Frontier Justice* (Norman: University of Oklahoma Press, 1949), 278 (quotation 3). Law enforcement officials' inability to locate suspects and witnesses figured prominently in the England family murder case.

41. Carrigan, *Lynching Culture,* 108.

42. Carrigan, *Lynching Culture,* 108.

43. Michael Ariens, *Lone Star Law: A Legal History of Texas* (Lubbock: Texas Tech University Press, 2011), 54, 225.

Chapter 3

1. *Merriam-Webster Online Dictionary,* s.v. "Dutchman" (accessed April 4, 2013), http://www.merriam-webster.com/dictionary/dutchman; Young County, TX, 1857–85 Tax Rolls, Reel 1, TSLAC; 1867 Texas Voter Registration Lists, Montague County, Reel 9, Entry No. 148, 9, TSLAC; Ely, *Texas Frontier and the Butterfield Overland Mail,* 127–29, 375. I also visited Ben Krebs's gravesite in Newport Cemetery, Lone Grove, OK, on January 16, 2013.

2. "Proffitt and Proffitt Crossing, TX," Quadrangle Topographic Maps and Aerial Photographs, MapTech, http://www.richardsonscharts.com; 1860 U.S. Federal Census, Young County, TX, M653, R1308, 6, NA; Ely, *Texas Frontier and the Butterfield Overland Mail,* 127–29, 375.

3. Carrie J. Crouch, *A History of Young County*, 2nd ed. (Austin: Texas State Historical Association, 1956), 91; 1860 U.S. Federal Census, Young County, TX, M653, R1308, 6, NA; Ely, *Texas Frontier and the Butterfield Overland Mail*, 127–29, 375.

4. Young County, TX, 1857–85 Tax Rolls, Reel 1, TSLAC; 1867 Texas Voter Registration Lists, Montague County Reel 9, Entry No. 148, 408, TSLAC; Montague County, TX, 1858–89 Tax Rolls, Reel 1, TSLAC; Patricia Adkins Rochette, *Bourland in North Texas and Indian Territory during the Civil War* (Broken Bow, OK: Author, 2005), 1:A-318.

5. Ely, *Texas Frontier and the Butterfield Overland Mail*, 127–29, 375; 1860 U.S. Federal Census, Montague County, TX, M653, R1301, 72, NA; 1870 U.S. Federal Census, Montague County, TX, M593, R1599, 5, NA; 1880 U.S. Federal Census, Montague County, TX, T9, R1320, 6, NA; 1900 U.S. Federal Census, Chickasaw Nation, Indian Territory, T623, R1850, ED 176, Sheet 10, NA; Texas Marriage Collection, 1851–1900, Ancestry.com, http://search.ancestry.com/cgi-bin/sse.dll?db=TX marriageindex-&h=446413&indiv=try&o_vc=Record:OtherRecord&rhSource=7163 (accessed April 10, 2013). Wiley Blount Savage's first marriage was to Mary A. Carney, who died in 1850. Among Wiley and Mary's children were Robert Savage and Thomas N. Savage. Wiley Savage married his second wife, Rhoda Taylor, on June 16, 1857, in Cooke County, TX, a marriage that lasted seven years until Wiley's death. Over the years, there has been some confusion regarding Eliza Ann "Rhoda" Taylor Savage Krebs. Some people have incorrectly assumed that there were two different women: Eliza Ann Taylor (later Eliza Ann Savage) and Rhoda Ann Krebs. In fact, these names refer to one woman. In 1869, Rhoda Krebs testified that her father was William Hampton Taylor and that William Barnett "Bill" Taylor was her brother. See Rhoda Krebs testimony, State of Texas, County of Montague, William H. Taylor Inquest, January 30, 1869, Letters Received of the Department of Texas, the District of Texas, and the Fifth Military District, 1865–70, M1193, R22, NA (hereafter William H. Taylor Inquest). In 1877, Rhoda Krebs testified that another of her brothers was Aaron Kendrick Taylor, the youngest son of William Hampton Taylor and Jane Barnett Taylor. See "A. K. Taylor v. The State, 1877," in Jackson and Jackson, *Cases Argued and Adjudged in the Court of Appeals*, 3:182. In 1879, Thomas N. Savage testified that he was a stepson of Rhoda Krebs by her first husband, Wiley Savage. See "Ben Krebs v. The State, 1880," in Jackson and Jackson, *Cases Argued and Adjudged in the Court of Appeals*, 8:19. In 1906, Thomas Savage's brother, Robert Savage, discussed his father Wiley's marriage to Rhoda A. Taylor. See B. B. Paddock, *History and Biographical Record of North and West Texas* (Chicago: Lewis Publishing, 1906), 2:152–53.

6. 1850 U.S. Federal Census, Rusk County, TX, M432, R914, 249B, NA; 1870 U.S. Federal Census, Montague County, TX, M593, R1599, 5, NA; Young County, TX, 1857–85 Tax Rolls, Reel 1, TSLAC; Marvin F. London, *Famous Court Cases of Montague County* (Saint Jo, TX: SJT Printers, 1992), 25 (quotation). London's work contains some factual errors and should be used with caution. Corroboration is recommended.

7. William H. Taylor Inquest, January 30, 1869, testimonies of Benjamin Krebs and Rhoda Krebs.

8. William H. Taylor Inquest, Thomas N. Savage testimony and deposition (quotations).

9. William H. Taylor Inquest, Rhoda Krebs testimony; Benjamin Krebs affidavit (quotations).

10. William H. Taylor Inquest, Benjamin Krebs affidavit (quotations 1–3), Thomas N. Savage affidavit (quotations 4–6).

11. William H. Taylor Inquest, Benjamin Krebs affidavit; Maj. Robert Murray Morris, Sixth Cavalry Headquarters, Fort Richardson, TX, to Lt. Louis V. Caziarc, AAG, Fifth Military District, February 14, 1869, Fort Richardson, TX, Entry 1, Letters Sent, 1868–78, Vol. 1, RG 393, Part 5; Col. James Oakes, Sixth Cavalry Headquarters, to Capt. C. E. Morse, AAG, Fifth Military District, May 30, 1869, and John Stroud, Montague County Sheriff, to Col. James Oakes, May 28, 1869, both in Letters Received, Correspondence of the Office of Civil Affairs of the District of Texas, Fifth Military District, and the Department of Texas, 1867–70, M1188, R15, NA; London, *Famous Court Cases of Montague County*, 25–26.

12. Oakes to Morse, May 30, 1869, and E. B. Turner, Attorney General's Office, Austin, TX, to Capt. C. E. Morse, June 20, 1869, and Hardin Hart, Seventh Judicial District of the State of Texas, Montague County, TX, to Brevet General James Oakes, May 24, 1869, all in Letters Received, Correspondence of the Office of Civil Affairs of the District of Texas, Fifth Military District, and the Department of Texas, 1867–70, M1188, R15, NA.

13. 1870 U.S. Federal Census, Montague County, TX, M593, R1599, 16, NA; Louis F. Fisch affidavit, Montague, TX, October 23, 1894, in Ben Krebs and James Preston Applications for Pardons, Texas Secretary of State Executive Clemency Records, Box 2-9/410, TSLAC (hereafter KPCF). Another brother of Bill Taylor's, George, served in the same Texas Ranger outfit as Bill, Capt. G. W. Campbell's Montague Company, which was stationed in Clay County on the Little Wichita River. See William Barnett Taylor Pension File no. C2581773, Veterans Administration, NA, National Personnel Records Center, St. Louis, MO (hereafter WBTPF).

14. W. A. Morris affidavit, Montague, TX, October 27, 1894; E. G. Douglass to J. S. Hogg, Sherman, TX, October 30, 1894 (quotation 1); Louis F. Fisch affidavit, Montague, TX, October 23, 1894, KPCF; James B. Gillett, *Fugitives from Justice: The Notebook of Texas Ranger Sergeant James B. Gillett* (Austin, TX: State House Press, 1997), 83 (quotation 2); Texas Governor James Hogg statement, November 28, 1894, published in *Austin American Statesman*, December 5, 1894 (quotation 3). Bill Taylor was also described as having auburn hair, blue eyes, and a fair complexion.

15. Montague County, TX, 1858–89 Tax Rolls, Reel 1, TSLAC; File Notes for Montague County, Wiley B. Savage Abstract No. 677, GLO; Montague County Commissioners Court, Minutes, Book A, Police Court, March 2, 1873, 13.

16. File Notes for Montague County, Thomas N. Savage Abstract No. 674, and William H. Taylor Abstract No. 738, GLO.

17. 1850 U.S. Federal Census, Jefferson County, IL, M432, R110, 314, NA; 1860 U.S. Federal Census, Williamson County, IL, M653, R239, 1057, NA; 1870 U.S. Federal Census, Grayson County, TX, NA, M593, R1588, 52; "Illinois Marriages, 1790–1860," Ancestry .com; "Texas County Marriage Index, 1837–1977," Ancestry.com; 1867 Grayson County Voter List, Texas Voter Registration Lists, 1867–1869, Reel 5, and Grayson County, TX,

1846–1878 Tax Rolls, Reel 1, and Montague County, TX, 1858–1889 Tax Rolls, Reel 1, TSLAC. Selena Taylor England's name appears as "Salena," "Salina," and "Celina" in some records. The 1850 census lists Selena as "Helena," born in Kentucky in 1821. The 1860 census lists her as "Sarah," born in Kentucky in 1811. The 1870 census lists her as "Celina" born in Kentucky in 1820. In the text I have estimated her age as fifty-six years in 1876. William England was born on April 25, 1794 in Goochland County, Virginia.

18. 1850 U.S. Federal Census, Franklin County, AR, M432, R26, 281, NA; 1860 U.S. Federal Census, Franklin County, AR, M653, R41, 353, NA; 1880 U.S. Federal Census, Madison County, AR, T9, R50, 27, NA; Franklin County Township Maps, Madison County, AR Genealogical and Historical Society Archives.

19. 1860 U.S. Federal Census, Montague County, TX, M653, R1301, 85, NA; Private William G. Music, Texas Ranger and Texas State Troops Muster Roll Index Cards, 1838–1900, TSLAC; Montague County, TX, 1858–1889 Tax Rolls, Reel 1, TSLAC; Rochette, *Bourland in North Texas*, 1:A-219.

20. 1860 U.S. Federal Census, Washington County, IL, M432, R131, 135, NA; 1860 U.S. Federal Census, Hunt County, TX, M653, R1298, 17, NA; 1870 U.S. Federal Census, Hunt County, TX, M593, R1593, 34, NA; John R. Music Texas Voter Registration, Hunt County, TX, November 20, 1869, Texas Voter Registration Lists, 1867–69, TSLAC; "Texas Marriage Index, 1824–2014," Ancestry.com; "Missouri Compiled Marriage Index, 1766–1983," Ancestry.com; Montague County, TX, 1858–1889 Tax Rolls, Reel 1, TSLAC. Luna and John Music named their first daughter Minerva Elizabeth after Luna's mother, their second daughter Louisa Belle after John's mother, and their son, William Daniel, after John's and Luna's fathers. The name Music is also spelled as "Musick" in some records.

21. File Notes for Montague County, T. N. Savage Survey, Abstract No. 674, GLO; entries for Thomas N. Savage, James Brooks, Billington Taylor, Salina [*sic*] and Saline [*sic*] England in Montague County, TX, 1858–1889 Tax Rolls, Reel 1, and Grayson County, TX, 1846–1878 Tax Rolls, Reel 1, TSLAC. William Granville Music is listed (as W. B. Music) in the Montague County, TX, tax rolls from 1861 to 1864, after which time he disappears from the rolls.

22. *The State of Texas v. John Musick* [*sic*], June 9, 1876, Montague County Criminal Minutes Book B, 140; *The State of Texas v. John Musick*, August 8, 1876, Montague County Criminal Court Minutes Book 1, 14; *The State of Texas v. Ben Krebs*, State Docket, Montague County Court Book, August, September, and October 1876, Terms, 6–7, 11–12; "*Ben Krebs v. The State*, 1880," in Jackson and Jackson, *Cases Argued and Adjudged in the Court of Appeals*, 8:21–22.

23. *The State of Texas v. Ben Krebs*, State Docket, Montague County Court Book; "*A. K. Taylor v. The State*, 1877," in Jackson and Jackson, *Cases Argued and Adjudged in the Court of Appeals*, 3:187.

24. "*A. K. Taylor v. The State*, 1877," 187.

25. *The State of Texas vs. Ben Krebs et al.*, Murder, a True Bill, signed, William Broaddus, foreman of the Grand Jury, filed October 31, 1876, Krebs and Preston Case File

No. 614/971, Box 323, Cooke County District Court, Criminal Cases; *The State of Texas vs. James Preston et al.*, Murder, and *The State of Texas vs. A. K. Taylor*, Murder, Grand Jury Indictments, Montague County Criminal Minutes, Book B, October 31, 1876, 173–75, November 3, 1876, 182–84, November 7, 1876, 188, and November 9, 1876, 203; *Galveston Daily News*, November 30, 1876.

26. *Galveston Daily News*, November 30, 1876; Krebs and Preston Case File No. 614/971, Box 323, Cooke County District Court, Criminal Cases; Montague County District Court, Criminal Minutes Book B, November 10, 1876, 192, and November 11, 1876, 205–6. A native of Tennessee, Finis E. Piner moved to Denton, TX, in 1864. He served as a state district attorney (1873–76), as a Texas state senator (1876–79), and as a state district judge (1884–88). See "Legislative Reference Library, Texas Legislators: Past and Present," https://lrl.texas.gov/mobile/memberDisplay.cfm?memberID=4400 (accessed November 21, 2018); *Biographical Souvenir of the State of Texas* (Chicago: F. A. Battey & Co., 1889), 674. Aaron Taylor was tried seven months after Krebs, on June 11, 1877, and James Preston's trial was held the following month, on July 9, 1877. The principals involved, and the evidence presented at Krebs's, Preston's, and Taylor's trials were much the same, with only a few notable differences.

27. *The State of Texas vs. Ben Krebs*, October Term 1876, Defendant's Bill of Exceptions, Bill of Exceptions No. 4, November 14, 1876, Krebs and Preston Case File No. 614/971, Box 323, Cooke County District Court, Criminal Cases; "*A. K. Taylor v. The State*, 1877," in Jackson and Jackson, *Cases Argued and Adjudged in the Court of Appeals*, 3:180–81.

28. "*A. K. Taylor v. The State*, 1877," 180.

29. "*A. K. Taylor v. The State*, 1877," 181.

30. "*A. K. Taylor v. The State*, 1877," 181.

31. "*A. K. Taylor v. The State*, 1877," 178, 179 (quotation).

32. "*A. K. Taylor v. The State*, 1877," 179. Blood type identification was discovered just after 1900. See Kirsty Strawbridge, "The History of Blood Types," https://bigpictureeducation.com/history-blood-types (accessed November 22, 1018). While there was some initial progress made in ballistics testing in England during the nineteenth century, the science did not come into its own until the early 1900s. Lisa Steele, "Ballistics," in *Science for Lawyers*, ed. Eric York Drogin (Chicago: American Bar Association, 2008), 1–30.

33. "*A. K. Taylor v. The State*, 1877," 180.

34. "*A. K. Taylor v. The State*, 1877," 180. Again, while Stinson could state that the unused pistol balls he found were of the same caliber, he could not prove that the Colt Navy Revolver recovered from the Krebs home was used in the murders. It should also be noted that Colt Navy Revolvers were very common during this period.

35. "*A. K. Taylor v. The State*, 1877," 182.

36. "*A. K. Taylor v. The State*, 1877," 182, 184.

37. "*A. K. Taylor v. The State*, 1877," 184.

38. "*A. K. Taylor v. The State*, 1877," 185.

39. "*A. K. Taylor v. The State*, 1877," 182.

40. "*A. K. Taylor v. The State*, 1877," 187.
41. "*A. K. Taylor v. The State*, 1877," 3:182–83; "*Ben Krebs v. The State*, 1880," 8:22. Following the death of his wife, Martha, in February 1876, James Preston moved to Sandy, a community near present-day Bowie, TX.
42. "*A. K. Taylor v. The State*, 1877," 182–83. The times cited are approximations. On August 26, the sun currently sets in Texas at around 8 P.M. (Central Standard Time). Time zones were not implemented in the United States until November 1883. See, "Why Do We Have Time Zones?" *Time and Date.com*, https://www.timeanddate .com/time/time-zones-history.html (accessed November 23, 2018).
43. "*A. K. Taylor v. The State*, 1877," 183.
44. "*A. K. Taylor v. The State*, 1877," 183–84 (quotation), 188.
45. "*A. K. Taylor v. The State*, 1877," 3:171 (quotation 1), 187–88; "*Ben Krebs v. The State*, 1880," 8:22 (quotation 2).
46. "*A. K. Taylor v. The State*, 1877," 187 (quotation 1), 188 (quotations 2 and 3).
47. "*A. K. Taylor v. The State*, 1877," 3:188; *The State of Texas vs. Ben Krebs*, October Term 1876, Defendant's Bill of Exceptions, Bill of Exceptions No. 3, November 14, 1876, Krebs and Preston Case File No. 614/971, Box 323, Cooke County District Court, Criminal Cases (quotation).
48. Judge J. A. Carroll, Instructions to the Jury, *The State of Texas vs. Ben Kribbs* [*sic*], November 11, 1876, Krebs and Preston Case File No. 614/971, Box 323, Cooke County District Court, Criminal Cases.
49. *Galveston Daily News*, November 23, 1876 (quotation 1); Trial Transcript, *State vs. Ben Krebs et al.*, District Court Term October 31, 1876, filed June 30, 1877, Krebs and Preston Case File No. 614/971, Box 323, Cooke County District Court, Criminal Cases (quotation 2). Former criminal lawyer and author Bill Neal notes that frontier juries of this period were not very sophisticated. They were "considerably more credulous . . . and gullible—and much more susceptible to . . . maudlin and . . . melodramatic appeals. . . . Emotion trumped evidence every time." Neal, *Getting Away with Murder*, 16. A number of people connected to the England murder case mentioned that Montague County Attorney Avery Lenoir Matlock played upon the fears of terrified residents, deliberately stoking local outrage and hysteria during the courtroom trials.
50. Montague County District Court, Criminal Minutes Book B, November 11, 1876, 205 (quotation), and November 14, 1876, 204; Trial Transcript, *State vs. Ben Krebs et al.*, District Court Term October 31, 1876, filed June 30, 1877, Krebs and Preston Case File No. 614/971, Box 323, Cooke County District Court, Criminal Cases; Montague County Deed Record Book E, November 7, 1876, 58–59.
51. *Graham Leader*, October 7, 1876 (quotation 1); *Dallas Herald*, November 25, 1876; *Galveston Daily News*, November 28, 1876 (quotation 2).
52. *Graham Leader*, October 7, 1876; *Galveston Daily News*, October 24, 1876, and November 28, 1876 (quotation); *Dallas Herald*, November 25, 1876.
53. Edward Franklin Bates, *History and Reminiscences of Denton County* (Denton, TX: Terrill Wheeler Printing, 1976), 147, 148 (quotation 1); *Dallas Herald*, November 25, 1876; *Galveston Daily News*, November 28, 1876 (quotations 2 and 3), November 22,

1879. Sixteenth Judicial District Judge Joseph Alexander Carroll, presiding judge during all five England murder trials, also presided over the trials of Andrew and George Brown in Denton during March 1878. The trials ended in guilty verdicts, the pair was hung in Denton on November 21, 1879, and subsequently buried in Denton's Oakwood Cemetery.

Chapter 4

1. *Ben Kribs [sic] v. The State*, Cause 51/91, November 24, 1877, Texas Court of Appeals Minutes, Vol. 211-027, Tyler, 1876–82, 139, Records Accession 1993/088, TSLAC; "*Ben Krebs v. The State*, 1877," in Jackson and Jackson, *Cases Argued and Adjudged in the Court of Appeals*, 3:358, 361–62.

2. *Ben Kribs v. The State*, Cause 51/91, TSLAC; "*Ben Krebs v. The State*, 1877," in Jackson and Jackson, *Cases Argued and Adjudged in the Court of Appeals*, 3:358, 361, 362 (quotation).

3. Montague County District Court, Criminal Minutes Book B, June 15, 1877, 291; "*A. K. Taylor v. The State*, 1877," in Jackson and Jackson, *Cases Argued and Adjudged in the Court of Appeals*, 3:202.

4. "*A. K. Taylor v. The State*, 1877," 3:171; *A. K. Taylor v. The State*, Cause 126, November 28, 1877, Texas Court of Appeals Minutes, Vol. 211-027, Tyler 1876–78, 142, Record Accession 1993/088, TSLAC; Montague County District Court, Criminal Minutes Book B, June 15, 1877, 291; Montague County Deed Record Book A, September 25, 1869, 285; Montague County Deed Record Book D, September 27, 1877, 140–41. As one of the Taylor children, Aaron Kendrick Taylor had inherited a one-seventh share in the William H. Taylor Survey, which he transferred to Grigsby & Willis law firm in September 1877.

5. Montague County District Court, Criminal Minutes Book B, June 13, 1878, 418 (quotation), 419; "*A. K. Taylor v. The State*, 1877," 3:202; A. K. Taylor Convict Record & Ledger Data Form, Texas State Penitentiary Records, TSLAC.

6. Montague County District Court, Criminal Minutes Book B, June 11, 1877, 262–63, and June 14, 1877, 289; "*James Preston v. The State*, 1878," in A. M. Jackson and A. M. Jackson Jr., *Cases Argued and Adjudged in the Court of Appeals of the State of Texas* (St. Louis, MO: Gilbert Book Co., 1879), 4:188.

7. "*James Preston v. The State*, 1878," 4:188; Montague County District Court, Criminal Minutes Book B, June 11, 1877, 262–63, and June 14, 1877, 289. As part of the change of venue to Gainesville, Judge Carroll ordered that all papers relating to the Krebs and Preston cases be transferred to the Cooke County Courthouse in Gainesville by Monday, July 2, 1877.

8. "*James Preston v. The State*, 1878," 4:187; "*Ben Krebs v. The State*, 1880," 8:16–17.

9. *James Preston v. State of Texas*, Cause 51/91, November 24, 1877, Texas Court of Appeals Minutes, Vol. 211-027, Tyler 1876–82, 123, Record Accession 1993/088, TSLAC; Montague County Deed Record Book E, October 5, 1876, 60–62.

10. "*James Preston v. The State*, 1878," in Jackson and Jackson, *Cases Argued and Adjudged in the Court of Appeals*, 4:194, 195 (quotation), 196.

11. *"James Preston v. The State, 1878,"* 4:195.

12. *"James Preston v. The State, 1878,"* 4:201–2.

13. *"James Preston v. The State, 1878,"* 4:201–2.

14. *"James Preston v. The State, 1878,"* 4:202.

15. *"James Preston v. The State, 1880,"* in Jackson and Jackson, *Cases Argued and Adjudged in the Court of Appeals,* 8:31–32; *Austin Weekly Statesman,* October 13, 1892; "Chronological Index of Texas Court of Criminal Appeals, 1836–1986," *Tarlton Law Library,* https://tarltonapps.law.utexas.edu/justices/index/criminal_appeals_chrono (accessed November 26, 2018); *James Preston v. State of Texas,* Cause 664, February 14, 1880, Texas Court of Appeals Minutes, TSLAC.

16. *"James Preston v. The State, 1880,"* 8:34 (quotation 1), 34–35 (quotation 2), 35 (quotation 3); "Chronological Index of Texas Court of Criminal Appeals," *Tarlton Law Library.* George W. Clark served less than a year on the court of appeals before resigning in October 1880 to return to his private law practice in Waco. Ironically, his successor on the court was none other than James Mann Hurt, one of Preston's defense attorneys. Hurt became presiding justice of the court of appeals in 1892.

17. *"James Preston v. The State, 1880,"* 8:35.

18. *"James Preston v. The State, 1880,"* 8:35, 36, 38 (quotations 1–3, respectively).

19. *"James Preston v. The State, 1880,"* 8:38 (quotation 1), 39 (quotation 2).

20. *"James Preston v. The State, 1880,"* 8:39.

21. *Galveston Daily News,* February 18, 1879; *San Antonio Daily Express,* February 22, 1879.

22. *"Ben Krebs v. The State, 1880,"* 8:16, 21–22; "Chronological Index of the Texas Court of Appeals, 1836–1986," *Tarlton Law Library* (accessed August 5, 2018); Montague County Deed Record Book F, February 11, 1878, 417–18.

23. *"Ben Krebs v. The State, 1880,"* 8:2 (quotation), 16, 21–22, 27.

24. *"Ben Krebs v. The State, 1880,"* 8:27.

25. Michael Ariens, email to author, September 11, 2019.

26. Michael Ariens, email, September 11, 2019.

27. Aviva A. Orenstein, "Her Last Words: Dying Declarations and Modern Confrontation Jurisprudence," *Maurer School of Law Digital Depository,* Indiana University, https://www.repository.law.indiana.edu/facpub/6 (accessed March 13, 2019), 1416 (quotations 1 and 2); Timothy T. Lau, "Reliability of Dying Declaration Hearsay Evidence," *American Criminal Law Review,* Vol. 55:373 (2018), 375; Robert H. Klugman, "Some Factors Affecting the Admissibility of Dying Declarations," *Journal of Criminal Law and Criminology,* Vol. 39 (Issue 5, 1949), https://scholarlycommons.law.northwestern.edu/jclc (accessed March 13, 2019), 646.

28. Orenstein, "Her Last Words," 1425–26, 1427 (quotation).

29. *"Ben Krebs v. The State, 1880,"* in Jackson and Jackson, *Cases Argued and Adjudged in the Court of Appeals,* 8:29 (quotations 1 and 2), 29–30 (quotation 3).

30. *"Ben Krebs v. The State, 1880,"* 8:30.

31. *Galveston Daily News,* May 1, 1880.

32. *Galveston Daily News,* May 1, 1880.

Chapter 5

1. Ariens, *Lone Star Law*, 219–20; *James Preston v. State of Texas*," Cause 664, February 14, 1880, and *Ben Krebs v. State of Texas*," Cause 665, February 14, 1880, both in Texas Court of Appeals Minutes, Volume 211-027, Tyler 1876–1882, 362, Accession 1993/088 Records, TSLAC.
2. Michael Ariens, interview with author, August 20, 2015, San Antonio, TX (quotation). Regarding the reluctance of appellate judges in overturning jury verdicts, Ariens explains,

> Only a guilty verdict could be appealed, and appellate courts rarely second-guessed the factual findings implicitly made in assessing a verdict of guilty. What appellate courts of the late nineteenth century regularly second-guessed were the legal rulings made by trial courts, including errors in the admission of evidence and providing jury instructions, to errors in the indictments and verdict form. And the Texas Court of Appeals, with its 65 percent reversal rate, was one of the most exacting and demanding appellate courts in the nation. Because it was rare for trial courts to conduct trials without making some legal error, a good lawyer could usually find some way to give the Texas Court of Appeals a legal reason to reverse the conviction. After Krebs and Preston were convicted a second time, they again appealed. Although some legal errors might remain from the first conviction, the opportunity given the trial court of a second chance to conduct the trial lessened the likelihood that the trial court would make some reversible legal error. Even when an appellate court was offered some compelling evidence of innocence, evidence that would give an objective observer pause, the Texas Court of Appeals was unlikely to look seriously at other credible scenarios or suspects. That was the job of the jury, as informed by the lawyers for the accused. The adversary system gave significant authority and responsibility to the lawyers for the state and the accused to bring evidence and alternate scenarios to the jury for its assessment whether the prosecution had proved the guilt of the defendants beyond a reasonable doubt. Even when an appellate court expressed doubts about the defendant's guilt it was rare for it to overrule a jury and conclude the defendant could not as a matter of law be guilty of the crime charged. (Michael Ariens email to author, September 11, 2019)

3. *Denison Daily News*, April 22, 1880; *Galveston Daily News*, May 1, 1880.
4. *Denison Daily News*, April 23, 1880 (quoting the *Galveston Daily News*).
5. Governor O. M. Roberts, proclamations commuting Krebs's and Preston's death sentences, April 24, 1880, Krebs and Preston Case File No. 614/971, Box 323, Cooke County District Court, Criminal Cases; Roberts to Cunningham and Ellis, Austin, TX, April 24, 1880, Governor Oran Milo Roberts Papers, Box 301-121, TSLAC. Regarding commutations and pardons, the Texas legislature created the Texas Board of Pardon

Advisers in 1893 to help the governor manage the increasing number of applications for executive clemency. The board made recommendations to the governor, but up until 1936, the governor had sole discretion in the awarding of executive clemency. After much controversy about pardon abuses by several governors, voters in 1936 amended the state constitution, stripping the governor of this power and giving it to the Texas Board of Pardons and Paroles, a politically independent body. See TSLAC, "Pardons and Paroles," https://www.tsl.texas.gov/exhibits/prisons/inquiry/pardons .html (accessed February 4, 2019); Stuart A. MacCorkle, "Pardoning Power in Texas," *Southwestern Social Science Quarterly* 15, no. 3 (December 1934), 219; Texas Board of Pardons and Paroles, *Handbook on Parole, Mandatory Supervision, and Executive Clemency* (Austin: Texas Board of Pardons and Paroles, 1978), 5; Yen Bui and Jeanette L. Jordan, "Amnesty and Pardon," *Encyclopedia of Criminology and Criminal Justice*, January 2014, https://onlinelibrary.wiley.com/doi/full/10.1002/9781118517383 .wbeccj056 (accessed February. 4, 2019).

6. L. Spain, Governor's Clerk, to the Sheriff of Cooke County, Gainesville, TX, April 26, 1880, Roberts Papers, Box 301-121, TSLAC.

7. Gov. O. M. Roberts's reasons for commuting Krebs's and Preston's sentences, April 24, 1880, KPCF.

8. Roberts's reasons for commuting Krebs's and Preston's sentences.

9. Michael Ariens, interview with author; Aragorn Storm Miller, "Joseph Alexander Carroll," in *Handbook of Texas Online*, https://tshaonline.org/handbook/online/articles/fcafd (accessed August 9, 2018); "The Exchange National Bank of Denton, Texas," in *The History of Denton County, Texas*, http://www.dentonhistory.net/page93/ (accessed August 10, 2018). After leaving the bench, Joseph Alexander Carroll became president of the Exchange National Bank in Denton, TX. He served as president from 1881 until his death in October 1891.

10. *Galveston Daily News*, April 30, 1880.

11. *Fort Griffin Echo*, May 8, 1880 (quotation 1); *Galveston Daily News*, April 30, 1880 (quotation 2).

12. *Galveston Daily News*, April 30, 1880, and May 1, 1880; *Denison Daily News*, May 1, 1880. Although Confederate authorities in Cooke County executed more than forty persons during the Great Hanging in Gainesville in October 1862 (forty hanged and two shot while trying to escape), many people have always viewed these killings as extralegal. For more on the Great Hanging, see chapter 2.

13. *Denison Daily News*, May 1, 1880.

14. *Galveston Daily News*, May 1, 1880 (quotation 1); *Denison Daily News*, May 1, 1880 (quotation 2).

15. *Galveston Daily News*, May 1, 1880 (quotations 1 and 2); *Denison Daily News*, May 1, 1880 (quotation 3). The Denison paper gave the clergyman's name as Reverend Hening but may have been referring to Gainesville pastor Rev. F. A. Heuring. See Ben Krebs to Reverend Heuring, printed in *Denison Daily News* (quoting the *Gainesville Hesperian*), August 25, 1880.

16. *Dallas Daily Herald*, April 27, 1880; Ford Dixon, "Oran Milo Roberts," in *Handbook of Texas Online*, https://tshaonline.org/handbook/online/articles/fro18 (accessed August 17, 2018).

17. *Fort Griffin Echo*, May 8, 1880.

18. *Galveston Daily News*, May 16, 1880; *Dallas Daily Herald*, May 11, 1880.

19. *Denison Daily News*, July 14, 1880; *Fort Worth Democrat* editorial, reprinted in the *Brenham Daily Banner*, May 6, 1880.

20. *Denison Daily News*, May 5, 1880.

21. Thomas H. Murray to Gov. O. M. Roberts, Denton, TX, May 4, 1880, Roberts Papers, Box 2G66, Dolph Briscoe Center for American History.

22. Murray to Roberts, May 4, 1880.

23. Murray to Roberts, May 4, 1880. See also David Minor, "Thomas Elisha Hogg," in *Handbook of Texas Online*, https://tshaonline.org/handbook/online/articles/fho19 (accessed November 27, 2018).

24. W. H. Grigsby and Frank Willis to Governor Roberts, Montague, TX, August 16, 1880, Roberts Papers, Box 2G67, Dolph Briscoe Center for American History. This letter may have reaped important political dividends, for less than a year later, Roberts appointed Frank Willis as district judge of the Thirty-First Judicial District in the Texas Panhandle. See H. Allen Anderson, "Frank Willis," in *Handbook of Texas Online*, https://tshaonline.org/handbook/online/articles/fwiab (accessed November 27, 2018).

25. Governor Oran Milo Roberts Pardon Register, Microfilm Rolls 12 and 15, Executive Record Books, 1835–1917, TSLAC.

26. *Galveston Daily News*, quoting the *Austin Daily Dispatch*, May 5, 1880.

Chapter 6

1. *Rules, Regulations, and By-Laws for the Government and Discipline of the Texas State Penitentiaries at Huntsville and Rusk, Texas* (Austin, TX: E. W. Swindells, 1882), 47; Aaron Kendrick Taylor Convict Register and Certificate of Prison Conduct, Texas Department of Criminal Justice, Texas Convict and Conduct Registers, 1875–1945, TSLAC.

2. Ben Krebs Convict Register and Certificate of Prison Conduct, Texas Department of Criminal Justice, Texas Convict and Conduct Registers, 1875–1945, TSLAC; *Denison Daily News* (quoting the *Gainesville Hesperian*), August 25, 1880 (quotation).

3. James Preston Convict Register and Certificate of Prison Conduct, Texas Department of Criminal Justice, Texas Convict and Conduct Registers, 1875–1945, TSLAC; Montague County Court Probate Minutes, 1873–84, Case No. 150, 1–194.

4. Donald R. Walker, *Penology for Profit: A History of the Texas Prison System, 1867–1912* (College Station: Texas A&M University Press, 1988), 11.

5. Walker, *Penology for Profit*, 11, 31, 46.

6. Walker, *Penology for Profit*, 51–52, 66, 189; *Texas State Penitentiaries, Superintendent and Financial Agent Reports for Two Years* (Austin, TX: Triplett & Hutchinson, 1888),

10, 47, 52; Edward Anson Hart, *Twenty-One Years in the Texas Penitentiary, or the Prison Life of Edward Anson Hart* (Stephenville, TX: Frank Leonard, 1900), 43.

7. Robert Perkinson, *Texas Tough: The Rise of America's Prison Empire* (New York: Metropolitan Books, 2010), 93.

8. Walker, *Penology for Profit*, 52, 75, 157–59. Recently, archaeologists uncovered a large convict graveyard at Sugar Land, Texas, where leased convicts who died working for Cunningham & Ellis were buried. See Meagan Flynn, "Bodies Believed to be Those of 95 Black Forced-Labor Prisoners from Jim Crow Era Unearthed in Sugar Land after One Man's Quest," *Washington Post* online, July 18, 2018, https://www.washingtonpost .com/news/morning-mix/wp/2018/07/18/bodies-of-95-black-forced-labor-prisoners -from-jim-crow-era-unearthed-in-sugar-land-after-one-mans-quest/?noredirect =on&utm_term=.10348a78396b (accessed December 10, 2018) (quotations); Joe South-ern, "Sugar Land's Dark History Revealed, Cemetery Yields Remains of Black Leased Convict Laborers," *Fort Bend Star* online, July 24, 2018, http://www.fortbendstar.com /sugar-lands-dark-history-revealed-cemetery-yields-remains-of-black-leased-convict -laborers/ (accessed December 10, 2018).

9. Walker, *Penology for Profit*, 143 (quotations 1 and 2); *Rules, Regulations and By-Laws*, 39–40; *Journal of the House of Representatives of the State of Texas*, 15th Legislature, 1st Sess. (Galveston, TX: Shaw and Blaylock, 1876), 397 (quotation 3).

10. Hart, *Twenty-One Years*, 24; *Journal of the House of Representatives*, 397 (quotation).

11. Walker, *Penology for Profit*, 38 (quotations 1 and 2); Hart, *Twenty-One Years*, 24; 1880 U.S. Federal Census, Walker County, TX, T9, R1331, ED152, 43, NA; 1900 U.S. Federal Census, Rusk State Penitentiary, Cherokee, TX, T623, ED 18, p. 90A, sheet 1, NA; *Reports of the Superintendent and Financial Agent of the Texas State Penitentiaries ending October 31, 1888* (Austin, TX: Eugene Von Boeckmann, 1889), 47; *Reports of the Superintendent and Financial Agent of the Texas State Penitentiaries ending October 31, 1894* (Austin, TX: Ben C. Jones, 1894), 62–63; M. Ezell to J. S. Hogg, Rusk, TX, August 10, 1893, KPCF. Marion Ezell, born in Tennessee in September 1853, started working in the Texas Prison system in 1870. In 1880, Ezell was working as a prison guard at the Huntsville Penitentiary. By 1888, Captain Ezell had risen to the position of underkeeper at the Rusk State Prison. After a short break, he again served as under-keeper at Rusk in 1892–94. By 1900, Ezell had married and had five children with his twenty-five-year-old wife, Lula. The underkeeper was the assistant superintendent's right-hand man and the second in command at the penitentiary. The underkeeper lived within the prison walls, was required to make daily visits to the inspect the convicts' cells, and supervised all overseers and guards. Lastly, he was required to inspect "the labor of convicts and see that all employees under him perform their duties, and that convicts are kept industriously employed." Paschal, *Digest of the Laws of Texas*, 404–5. As a side note, the 1900 census lists two other Ezells, Leo and Labron, working at the Rusk Penitentiary.

12. Gary Brown, *Texas Gulag: The Chain Gang Years, 1875–1925* (Plano, TX: Republic of Texas Books, 2002), 116 (quotation 1), 117–18 (quotation 2), 118 (quotation 3), 122.

13. Brown, *Texas Gulag*, 118–19.

14. Brown, *Texas Gulag*, 119 (quotation 1), 120 (quotation 2).

15. Brown, *Texas Gulag*, 43–53; Ethan Blue, "A Parody of the Law: Organized Labor, the Convict Lease, and Immigration in the Making of the Texas State Capitol," *Journal of Social History* 43, no. 4 (Summer 2010), 1033 (quotation).

16. Hart, *Twenty-One Years*, 24.

17. Walker, *Penology for Profit*, 38 (quotation 1); *Rules, Regulations and By-Laws*, 18 (quotations 2 and 3); Hart, *Twenty-One Years*, 45 (quotations 4 and 5).

18. Hart, *Twenty-One Years*, 45.

19. *Journal of the House of Representatives*, 401.

20. Hart, *Twenty-One Years*, 46.

21. Hart, *Twenty-One Years*, 46 (quotation 1); Walker, *Penology for Profit*, 140 (quotation 2); *Journal of the House of Representatives*, 275 (quotation 3).

22. *Journal of the House of Representatives*, 396 (quotation 1); Walker, *Penology for Profit*, 141 (quotation 2).

23. *Reports of the Superintendent and Financial Agent, 1888*, Exhibits 5, 7, 8, 43.

24. *Rules, Regulations and By-Laws*, 20, 38; *Reports of the Superintendent and Financial Agent, 1888*, Exhibit 6 (quotation); Andrew L. George, *The Texas Convict: Sketches of the Penitentiary, Convict Farms, and Railroads* (Marion, IL: Leader Print, 1895), 14; Hart, *Twenty-One Years*, 43; Sherri Knight, *Tom P's Fiddle: A True Texas Tale* (Minneapolis, MN: Langdon Street Press, 2008), 228.

25. *Rules, Regulations and By-Laws*, 39–40; George, *Texas Convict*, 13.

26. George, *Texas Convict*, 14; *Rules, Regulations and By-Laws*, 20, 38, 43; *Reports of the Superintendent and Financial Agent 1888*.

27. Aaron Kendrick Taylor Convict Register and Certificate of Prison Conduct, Texas Department of Criminal Justice, Texas Convict and Conduct Registers, 1875–1945, TSLAC; Thomas J. Goree to Governor L. S. Ross, Huntsville, TX, September 16, 1887, KPCF (quotation).

28. "Captain Joe Byrd Cemetery," *Texas Prison Museum*, http://txprisonmuseum.org/articles/cemetery.html (accessed December 24, 2016); *Journal of the House of Representatives*, 401 (quotation). The cemetery is named after Captain Joe Byrd, assistant warden of the Walls Unit, who began cleaning up the long-neglected graveyard in 1962. The oldest section of Peckerwood Hill, containing Taylor's and other anonymous graves, is located at the intersection of Sycamore Street and Bowers Boulevard in Huntsville.

29. James Preston and Ben Krebs Convict Registers and Certificates of Prison Conduct, Texas Department of Criminal Justice, Texas Convict and Conduct Registers, 1875–1945, TSLAC; Walker, *Penology for Profit*, 85–88.

30. *Reports of the Superintendent and Financial Agent, 1888*, 47 (quotation 1); *Reports of the Superintendent and Financial Agent of the Texas State Penitentiaries ending October 31, 1890* (Austin: Henry Hutchings, 1890), 36 (quotations 2 and 3).

31. *Reports of the Superintendent and Financial Agent, 1888*, 47 (quotation); *Reports of the Superintendent and Financial Agent, 1890*, 17.

32. *Reports of the Superintendent and Financial Agent, 1890*, 25 (quotation 1), Exhibit 10; Brown, *Texas Gulag*, 169 (quotations 2 and 3); Perkinson, *Texas Tough*, 118 (quotation 4).

33. Crawford & Crawford to Hon. O. M. Roberts, Dallas, TX, May 8, 1885, Roberts Papers, Box 2G66, Dolph Briscoe Center for American History.

Chapter 7

1. Crawford & Crawford to Hon. O. M. Roberts, Dallas, TX, May 8, 1885, Roberts Papers, Box 2G66, Dolph Briscoe Center for American History.

2. Crawford & Crawford to Roberts, May 8, 1885, and J. A. Carroll to Gov. Roberts, Denton, TX, May 12, 1885 (quotation), Roberts Papers, Box 2G66, Dolph Briscoe Center for American History.

3. *Dallas Morning News*, November 29, 1894.

4. Claude Elliott, "John Ireland," in *Handbook of Texas Online*, https://tshaonline.org/handbook/online/articles/firo1 (accessed November 30, 2018).

5. Governor John Ireland Pardon Register, Microfilm Rolls 12, 15, 16, and 17, Executive Record Books, 1835–1917, TSLAC.

6. W. C. Wolff to Gov. L. S. Ross, Dallas, TX, October 20, 1887, and October 22, 1887 (quotation), KPCF. W. C. Wolff was born in 1832 in Charleston, SC. See *Memorial and Biographical History of Dallas County* (Chicago: Lewis Publishing, 1892), 704–5.

7. Citizens of Montague County to Gov. L. S. Ross, Montague, TX, October 5, 1887, KPCF. Finis E. Piner, born in Tennessee on Dec. 3, 1837, was elected district judge for the Sixteenth Judicial District in 1884 and served until January 1888, when he retired to private law practice. Piner died on Dec. 13, 1900, and is buried in Odd Fellows Cemetery in Denton, Texas.

8. Texas State Penitentiaries, Certificates of Prison Conduct, Convicts 347 Krebs and 348 Preston, Thomas J. Goree, Supt., to Gov. S. L. Ross, Huntsville, TX, September 16, 1887, KPCF; W. C. Wolff to Gov. L. S. Ross, Dallas, TX, [no month or day] 1887, KPCF (quotation).

9. Mrs. L. B. Dickerson to Gov. L. S. Ross, Bowie, TX, September 5, 1887, KPCF. In 1887, W. C. Wolff wrote to Grayson County Sheriff R. L. May, seeking information on Harvey Taylor. May responded that Harvey had died in 1885 in Gordonsville, TX, but that his brother Isaac was still living. Wolff also wrote to the postmaster at Gordonsville, who told him that Harvey had been dead three years or longer. Two other brothers of Harvey's, Joe and Birch Taylor, were also deceased, but Joe Taylor's widow was still living in Montague County. R. L. May, Grayson County Sheriff, to W. C. Wolff, Sherman, TX, September 26, 1887, and W. C. Wolff to Postmaster at Gordonsville, TX, September 27, 1887, KPCF.

10. Mrs. L. B. Dickerson to Gov. L. S. Ross, Bowie, TX, September 5, 1887, KPCF.

11. J. W. Wayburn, acting deputy sheriff of Montague County, to Gov. L. S. Ross, Montague, TX, October 7, 1887, KPCF.

12. Wayburn to Ross, October 7, 1887.

13. W. C. Wolff to Gov. L. S. Ross, Dallas, TX, November 6, 1887, KPCF.

14. Wolff to Ross, November 6, 1887, KPCF.

15. Lucas F. Smith to Gov. L. S. Ross, Dallas, TX, November 16, 1887, KPCF.

16. Smith to Ross, November 16, 1887.

17. W. C. Wolff to Gov. L. S. Ross, Dallas, TX, [no day or month] 1887, KPCF.

18. Wolff to Ross, 1887 (quotation); Gov. Lawrence Sullivan Ross Pardon Register, Microfilm Rolls 13, 17, and 20, Executive Record Books, 1835–1917, TSLAC.

19. James Preston to O. M. Roberts, Rusk, TX, March 2, 1890, KPCF.

20. O. M. Roberts to Gov. S. L. Ross, Austin, TX, April 2, 1890, KPCF.

21. E. G. Douglass to Gov. James S. Hogg, Rusk, TX, November [no day] 1891, KPCF; Robert C. Cotner, "James Stephen Hogg," in *Handbook of Texas Online*, https://tshaonline.org/handbook/online/articles/fho17 (accessed December 2, 2018). See also "Elbridge Geary Douglass," in *Legislative Reference Library, Texas Legislators: Past & Present*, https://lrl.texas.gov/mobile/memberDisplay.cfm?memberID=3846 (accessed December 2, 2018). Elbridge Geary Douglass had been a state senator from Cooke and Grayson Counties for two years when Governor Ross tapped him in 1889 to become the new assistant superintendent of the state prison at Rusk. The Texas senate confirmed Douglass's appointment on January 23, 1889.

22. James Preston to Gov. J. S. Hogg, Rusk, TX, November 10, 1891, KPCF.

23. L. B. Dickerson Affidavit, Montague, TX, July 20, 1892, KPCF.

24. L. B. Dickerson Affidavit, July 20, 1892.

25. L. B. Dickerson Affidavit, July 20, 1892.

26. Montague County, File Notes for T. N. Savage Survey, Abstract No. 674, GLO; Entries for Thomas N. Savage, Salina [*sic*] and Saline [*sic*] England in Montague County, TX, 1858–89 Tax Rolls, Reel 1, TSLAC; L. B. Dickerson Affidavit, July 20, 1892, KPCF.

27. L. B. Dickerson Affidavit, July 20, 1892.

28. L. B. Dickerson Affidavit, July 20, 1892.

Chapter 8

1. W. J. Sparks to J. S. Hogg, Montague, TX, August 1, 1892, KPCF.

2. Sparks to Hogg, August 1, 1892.

3. William M. Walton to James S. Hogg, Austin, TX, August 2, 1892, and Walton to Hogg, Austin, TX, August 6, 1892, KPCF (quotation 1); Griffin Ford to J. S. Hogg, Bowie, TX, August 2, 1892, KPCF (quotation 2).

4. [Georgia Ann] Annie Krebs to J. S. Hogg, Lone Grove, Indian Territory, December 1, 1892, KPCF.

5. O. P. Taylor to Gov. James S. Hogg, Texarkana, TX, July 26, 1893, KPCF (quotation 1); Annie Krebs to J. S. Hogg December 1, 1892 (quotations 2 and 3).

6. Annie Krebs to J. S. Hogg, December 1, 1892.

7. Annie Krebs to former Gov. F. R. Lubbock, Lone Grove, Indian Territory, July 25, 1893 (quotations); and Annie Krebs to J. S. Hogg, Lone Grove, Indian Territory, July 25, 1893, KPCF.

8. O. P. Taylor to Board of Pardon Advisers, Texarkana, TX, July 26, 1893, KPCF.

9. Taylor to Board of Pardon Advisers, July 26, 1893.

10. M. Ezell to J. S. Hogg, Rusk, TX, August 10, 1893, KPCF.

11. O. M. Roberts to L. D. Brooks, Marble Falls, TX, November 23, 1893, KPCF.

12. Roberts to Brooks, November 23, 1893 (quotations). Roberts's handwritten commutation proclamation mentions Krebs's and Preston's cases "being before me upon application for commutation . . . as requested by the Judge [Carroll] and others." It makes no mention of a pardon. See O. M. Roberts, Commutation Proclamation for Ben Krebs and James Preston, Executive Office, Austin, TX, April 24, 1880, KPCF.

13. Roberts to Brooks, November 23, 1893.

14. Roberts to Brooks, November 23, 1893. In his letter to Brooks, Roberts did not disclose that both he and Carroll took steps to lobby Governor Ireland for a pardon in May 1885.

15. Roberts to Brooks, November 23, 1893.

16. Roberts to Brooks, November 23, 1893.

17. Roberts to Brooks, November 23, 1893.

18. James P. Gibson to F. R. Lubbock, Rusk, TX, November 25, 1893, KPCF.

19. James P. Gibson to F. R. Lubbock, Rusk, TX, November 26, 1893, KPCF.

20. Annie Krebs to James S. Hogg, Lone Grove, Indian Territory, December 2, 1893, and L. D. Brooks and F. R. Lubbock to James S. Hogg, Austin, TX, December 23, 1893, KPCF.

21. Brooks and Lubbock to Hogg, December 23, 1893.

22. Brooks and Lubbock to Hogg, December 23, 1893.

23. Brooks and Lubbock to Hogg, December 23, 1893.

24. Brooks and Lubbock to Hogg, December 23, 1893.

25. Brooks and Lubbock to Hogg, December 23, 1893.

26. Brooks and Lubbock to Hogg, December 23, 1893.

Chapter 9

1. "TX Governor, 1894," Our Campaigns, https://www.ourcampaigns.com/RaceDetail .html?RaceID=264397 (accessed December 15, 2018); Robert C. Cotner, "James Stephen Hogg," in *Handbook of Texas Online*, https://tshaonline.org/handbook/online/articles/ fho17 (accessed December 15, 2018).

2. E. G. Douglass to J. S. Hogg, Sherman, TX, October 30, 1894, KPCF.

3. Douglass to Hogg, October 30, 1894; C. F. McGrady Affidavit, Montague, TX, October 29, 1894, KPCF; "Robert Allen McGrady," *Find A Grave Index*, https:// search.ancestry.com/cgi-bin/sse.dll?dbid=60525&h=99736373&indiv=try&o_vc =Record:OtherRecord&rhSource=6742 (accessed December 17, 2018); 1880 U.S. Federal Census, Montague County, TX, T9, R1320, ED120, 12, NA.

4. Douglass to Hogg, October 30, 1894; W. A. Morris Affidavit, Montague, TX, October 27, 1894, KPCF. S. L. Newman, the Montague county clerk, told Douglass that McGrady was "a good honorable law-abiding citizen and his reputation for truth and veracity is good." S. L. Newman Affidavit, Montague, TX, October 27, 1894, KPCF.

5. Douglass to Hogg, October 30, 1894.

6. Douglass to Hogg, October 30, 1894; Brian Hart, "Red River Station," in *Handbook of Texas Online*, https://tshaonline.org/handbook/online/articles/hvr24 (accessed December 16, 2018).

7. "*Ben Krebs v. The State*, 1880," in Jackson and Jackson, *Cases Argued and Adjudged in the Court of Appeals*, 8:2.

8. Louis Fred Fisch Affidavit, Montague, TX, October 23, 1894 , KPCF (quotations); Douglass to Hogg, October 30, 1894. M. J. Davis, the Montague County district clerk, attached a note to Fisch's affidavit stating that he had known Fisch (a native of Switzerland like Krebs) for more than two decades, that Fisch "lived in the neighborhood of where the England murder was committed, for which Ben Krebs and Old Man Preston was [*sic*] convicted and are now serving life sentences in the penitentiary of this state, and that anything Mr. Fisch might say in regard to that matter or anything else is entitled to full credit as he is a man whose veracity has never been called into question." Statement of M. J. Davis, Montague County District Court Clerk, Montague, TX, October 25, 1894, KPCF.

9. Louis Fred Fisch Affidavit, October 23, 1894.

10. Louis Fred Fisch Affidavit, October 23, 1894.

11. Louis Fred Fisch Affidavit, October 23, 1894.

12. James M. Grigsby Affidavit, Montague, TX, October 27, 1894, KPCF (quotations); "James M. Grigsby," *Find A Grave*, https://www.findagrave.com/memorial/44484996/james-m-grigsby (accessed December 17, 2018); H. Allen Anderson, "Willis, Frank," in *Handbook of Texas Online*, https://tshaonline.org/handbook/online/articles/fwiab (accessed December 17, 2018).

13. James M. Grigsby Affidavit, October 27, 1894 (quotations); Thomas H. Murray to Gov. O. M. Roberts, Denton, TX, May 4, 1880, Roberts Papers, Box 2G66, Dolph Briscoe Center for American History; L. B. Dickerson Affidavit, Montague, TX, July 20, 1892, KPCF.

14. Gov. James S. Hogg, Ben Krebs and James Preston Pardon, Austin, TX, November 28, 1894, KPCF.

15. Hogg, Krebs and Preston Pardon, November 28, 1894.

16. L. B. Dickerson Affidavit, Montague, TX, July 20, 1892, and Hogg, Ben Krebs and James Preston Pardon, November 28, 1894.

17. Hogg, Krebs and Preston Pardon, November 28, 1894.

18. Hogg, Krebs and Preston Pardon, November 28, 1894. Governor Hogg used the spelling "Musick" throughout this document, but I have standardized to "Music" for continuity.

19. Hogg, Krebs and Preston Pardon, November 28, 1894 (quotation); Gov. James Stephen Hogg Pardon Register, Microfilm Rolls 13, 21, and 22, Executive Record Books, 1835–1917, TSLAC.

Chapter 10

1. *Galveston Daily News*, December 6, 1894.

2. *Galveston Daily News*, December 6, 1894.

3. *Gainesville Daily Hesperian*, November 30, 1894.

4. *Gainesville Daily Hesperian*, November 30, 1894.

5. *Galveston Daily News*, December 2, 1894.

6. *Galveston Daily News*, December 2, 1894.

7. *San Antonio Express*, quoted in *Galveston Daily News*, December 3, 1894; Brandi Grissom, "Rebuilding after Prison: Texas Has Spent $109 Million on the Wrongfully Convicted," *Dallas Morning News*, October 23, 2017, https://www.dallasnews.com/news /texas-legislature/2017/10/23/rebuilding-prison-texas-spent-109-million-wrongfully -convicted (accessed December 22, 2018) (quotation).

8. Grissom, "Rebuilding after Prison."

9. *San Antonio Express*, quoted in the *Galveston Daily News*, December 3, 1894; *Waco News*, quoted in *Galveston Daily News*, December 3, 1894.

10. *Galveston Daily News*, December 3, 1894.

11. *Austin Statesman*, quoted in the *Galveston Daily News*, December 8, 1894.

12. *Austin Statesman*, quoted in the *Galveston Daily News*, December 8, 1894.

13. *Galveston Daily News*, December 2, 1894.

14. 1900 U.S. Federal Census, Chickasaw Nation, Indian Territory, T63, R1850, 176, NA. Annie Krebs married Napoleon "Poley" Davidson on November 25, 1899. The marriage did not last. The 1910 and 1940 censuses record Poley as married to a different woman, Lucinda or Linda Davidson. See Carter County, OK, Marriage Records, 1890–1995, *Ancestry.com*, https://www.ancestry.com/interactive/61379/TH-1-9726– 29365-96?pid=64357507&backurl=http://search.ancestry.com/cgi-bin/sse.dll?dbid% 3D61379%26h%3D64357507%26indiv%3Dtry%260_vc%3DRecord:OtherRecord%26rh Source%3D7602&usePUB=true&usePUBJs=true (accessed December 23, 2018); 1910 U.S. Federal Census, Stephens County, OK, Ancestry.com, https://search.ancestry .com/cgi-bin/sse.dll?db=1910USCenIndex&indiv=try&h=156260860 (accessed December 23, 2018); 1940 U.S. Federal Census, Stephens County, OK, Ancestry.com, https://search.ancestry.com/cgi-bin/sse.dll?dbid=2442&h=89200755&indiv=try&o _vc=Record:OtherRecord&rhSource=7884 (accessed December 23, 2018); 1900 U.S Federal Census, Choctaw Nation, Indian Territory, Ancestry.com, https://search .ancestry.com/cgi-bin/sse.dll?db=1900usfedcen&indiv=try&h=75071061 (accessed December 23, 2018).

15. Ben Krebs's grave is in the Newport Cemetery near Lone Grove, OK. Rhoda and Annie Krebs are buried in the Duncan, OK, Cemetery. Despite an intensive search of all the cemeteries in Coal County, OK, including Lehigh and Coalgate, I was unable to find James Preston's grave. I was also unable to find a photograph of Preston. Lastly, a rigorous review of regional Oklahoma newspapers at the state history center in Oklahoma City failed to turn up a notice of James Preston's death. Preston's daughter-in-law, Vesta B. Preston, wife of son James Jr., and Preston's grandson, Earl, son of James Jr. and Vesta, are buried in the Wilson Cemetery in Township 1, not far from where the Preston home was in 1900. Vesta (born in June 1874) died in August 1901, and Earl (born in January 1901) died in October 1901. See *Daily Ardmorite*, February 24, 1901; Joyce E. Whatley Family Genealogy Research Book (given to the author by her daughter, Cheryl Rivera). Whatley was a relative who received much of her information directly from Winifred Preston. See also 1930 U.S. Federal Census, Tulsa County, OK, Ancestry.com, https://www.ancestry.com/interactive/6224/4661252_00690?pid =95291251&backurl=https://search.ancestry.com/cgi-bin/sse.dll?dbid%3D6224%26h%3

D95291251%26indiv%3Dtry%260_vc%3DRecord:OtherRecord%26rhSource%3D2548& treeid=&personid=&hintid=&usePUB=true&usePUBJs=true (accessed December 23, 2018).

16. William Preston Krebs, phone interview with the author, Claremore, OK, February 24, 2017.

17. William Preston Krebs, phone interview (quotation), and in-person interview, Claremore, OK, December 27, 2018; L. B. Dickerson Affidavit, Montague, TX, July 20, 1892, KPCF; 1850 Franklin County, AR, Township Map, and 1860 Madison County, AR, Township Map, Madison County, AR, Genealogical and Historical Society Archives; U.S. Federal Censuses: 1850, Franklin County, AR, M432, R26, 281, NA; 1860, Montague County, TX, M653, R1301, 72, NA; 1880, Franklin County, AR, T9, R50, ED105, 574D, NA; 1860, Hunt County, TX, M653, R1298, 17, NA; 1870, Hunt County, TX, M593, R1593, 34, NA; Texas Marriage Index, 1824–2014, Missouri Compiled Marriage Index, 1766–1983, Arkansas County Marriage Index, 1837–1957, and Texas Death Certificates, 1903–82, all at Ancestry.com. As for Luna Broderick Smith Music, after John Music abandoned her and their children in 1880, she met her fourth husband, Bonam Franklin Dickerson, in Wise County, TX. They married in 1881 and subsequently had three children. Luna died June 18, 1927, in Marble Falls, TX. Interestingly, before she married Bonam Dickerson, she and her children were living at the Wise County home of Charles Harris, a former brother-in-law. Charles Harris was the brother of James W. Harris, whom Luna married in August 1872, between her two marriages to John R. Music. Her nickname for much of her life was "Looney" a play on her given name, Luna.

18. Scott County, AR, Marriage Records, Book A, 86; W. A. Denton Affidavit, Scott County, AR, December 16, 1918, in "Scott County, AR, Affidavits," Scott County, AR, Historical and Genealogical Society Archives, 17, 64; Road District Overseers, Scott County, AR, Court Records, Book A, 571; 1882 Brawley Township Map, Scott County, AR, Historical and Genealogical Society Archives.

19. Scott County, AR, Marriage Records, Book A, 421; Scott County, AR, Judgment Docket, 1882–1891, 98; Scott County Civil Court Records, 1882–1901, Book 4, 276; 1900 U.S. Federal Census, Scott County, AR, T623, R75, ED108, 18. During his time in Scott County, AR, John R. Music also resided in Winfield, six miles east of Brawley. When he married his fourth wife, Olive, in 1888, he was living in Winfield, near Cross Creek Mountain, Jones Creek, and modern County Road 248. Brawley, AR, is now a ghost town on Jones Creek Road, just west of present-day Lake Hinkle.

20. William Preston Krebs phone interview, February 24, 2017 (quotations), and in-person interview, December 27, 2018.

21. William Preston Krebs, phone interview, February 24, 2017 (quotation 1), and in-person interview, December 27, 2018 (quotation 2). When questioned by census takers in the 1900, 1910, 1920, and 1930 federal censuses, Bill Taylor gave contradictory responses regarding where he and his parents were born.

22. William Barnett Taylor Pension File no. C2581773, Veterans Administration, National Personnel Records Center, NA, St. Louis, MO (hereafter WBTPF); Robert Hampton

Taylor Affidavit, Zora, MO, March 26, 1926, WBTPF. Robert Taylor said that Bill arrived at his farm in the same year as the Samuel J. Tilden versus Rutherford B. Hayes presidential election, which was in 1876. Bill Taylor's first wife, Julia Ann Stansbery, recalled that Bill showed up in Benton County during the summer of 1876. See Julia Ann Stansbery Affidavit, Sedalia, MO, March 26, 1926, WBTPF.

23. Julia Ann Stansbery Affidavits, Sedalia, MO, March 23 and 26, 1926; Special Investigator to Commissioner of Pensions, Kansas City, MO, March 30, 1926; Robert Hampton Taylor Affidavits, Zora, MO, March 25 and 26, 1926; Hiram Franklin Affidavit, Sedalia, MO, March 26, 1926; William Barnett Taylor Affidavit, Vinita, OK, July 17, 1925, all in WBTPF. According to Julia Ann Stansbery, the child she had with Bill Taylor in 1877, Lizzie, eventually married William Boatright and settled in Stover, Morgan County, MO.

24. William Barnett Taylor Affidavit, Vinita, OK, July 17, 1925, and Nancy Lucas Taylor to Director of Pensions, Veterans Bureau, September 30, 1934, both in WBTPF.

25. William Barnett Taylor Affidavits, Vinita, OK, July 17, 1925, and Craig County, OK, March 21, 1928, WBTPF. In his interview with T. Quinn Jones, Bill's brother Robert Hampton Taylor also withheld information about the Taylor family's time in Montague County, Texas. Robert was living in Montague County in 1869 when Bill killed their father. Like his brother Bill, Robert told Jones only that their father had died in Montague County. Additionally, Robert said nothing about the England murders or what happened to their sister Rhoda, their brother-in-law Ben Krebs, and their brother Aaron Kendrick Taylor. See Robert Hampton Taylor Affidavits, Zora, MO, March 25 and 26, 1926, WBTPF.

26. T. Quinn Jones, Report to Commissioner of Pensions, Kansas City, MO, March 30, 1926, WBTPF (quotation 1); T. Quinn Jones Report, Joplin, MO, May 6, 1926, WBTPF (quotations 2 and 3).

27. W. B. Taylor Death Certificate, Vinita, Craig County, OK, September 10, 1934; Nancy Taylor & Burckhalter Funeral Home to Veterans Administration, Claim for Burial Expenses, September 15, 1934; Nancy Taylor Affidavit Supporting Burial Claim, October 18, 1934; Public Voucher Questionnaire for Burial, Funeral, or Transportation of Veteran, Veterans Administration, October 24, 1934, WBTPF. Nancy Taylor's application for an Indian Wars widow's pension stated that she was almost blind and could not recognize her own children. She lived for another eleven years on a pension of $28.50 per month, which was eventually increased to $40 a month, until her death on December 28, 1945. She is buried next to her husband in Fairview Cemetery in Vinita, OK. See Nancy Taylor, Declaration for Widow's Pension—Indian Wars, November 24, 1934; Nancy Taylor Affidavit, Vinita, OK, December 31, 1934; Louis J. Johnston to Pension Bureau, Vinita, OK, March 22, 1944; Veterans Administration, Memorandum for File—Death of Beneficiary, January 12, 1946, WBTPF.

28. The April 27, 1880, issue of the *Galveston Daily News* bears consideration for its presentation of alternate scenarios and motives in the England family murders, albeit that their article has some flaws. The *News* reported that during the Krebs-Preston-Taylor trials, defense attorneys tried to present an alternative hypothesis that three

other men were the killers. This intriguing story mentions Ben Hall, a felonious associate of Bill Taylor's. Perhaps this "Ben Hall" is the Charles Hall mentioned in official records. The report also discusses a vigilante group operating in Montague County during this period. Although the prosecution called witnesses who testified that Krebs had threatened Isaiah Taylor, Selena England, and William England, no evidence was ever introduced showing that Krebs had threatened Susie Taylor prior to the slayings. The only statements tying Krebs to Susie's murder are Selena's dying declarations, made after the attack. The *News* article claimed that the defense attempted to present new evidence showing that Krebs had no motive to kill Susie, whereas a ne'er-do-well outlaw named Ben Hall did. Hall, who was enamored of Susie, was persistently thwarted in his pursuit of her by Selena England. The prosecution objected to the introduction of this evidence in court and District Judge Carroll sustained the objection. According to the *News*, defense attorneys alleged that in the 1870s Ben Hall had lived near the Englands in Grayson County. He began courting Susie Taylor and the two soon became engaged. Susie's brother Harvey supported Hall, but her mother, Selena, adamantly opposed the marriage. Selena was vindictive toward Hall and insisted that the engagement be called off, which greatly angered him. During this time, Hall was arrested for livestock theft. Susie's other brother, Isaiah, assisted Hall in posting bond, but subsequently turned Hall over to the local authorities "because he had publicly threatened to kill Susie if she did not cease the circulation of slanderous reports about him." Hall was tried, convicted, and sent to Huntsville. Another neighbor of the Englands in Whitesboro, Mr. Pierce, became upset over the family's shabby treatment of Hall. Pierce shared his feelings with Reverend England in a discussion that escalated into a heated argument. The next day Pierce's body was discovered lying in the road fifty yards from the England residence. "Suspicion attached to old man England and Pierce's brother swore vengeance against him. The [England] family, still under a cloud, moved a few months later to Montague County." Bill Taylor "had been a 'pard' of Hall in horse and cattle transactions of the kind [i.e., rustling] which sent the embittered and disappointed lover to the penitentiary. [William] England and Isaiah Taylor, shortly after their removal to Montague, joined the vigilantes. Bill Taylor was under a ban of the organization, being a notorious desperado and the murderer of his own father. On the day of the . . . [England] massacre Bill Taylor was seen in the country, accompanied by two men who answer the description of Hall and Pierce. Hall, two months before, had escaped from the penitentiary and rejoined Taylor in the wilds bordering Indian nation." According to the *News*, the defense theory was that during the attack on the England home, while Bill Taylor was covering Harvey Taylor with his revolver, Ben Hall "killed Isaiah for having surrendered him and taken part in his prosecution, [and] killed Mrs. England for having set her daughter against him, [while] Pierce shot and cut old man England's throat for having killed his brother, [and] Miss Susie was murdered by the man whose love she scorned [Hall], and Harvey was spared because he had favored the suit of Hall, was a friend of Pierce, and had refused to join the vigilantes. Be the theory false or true, the [England] case will be classed in the books among the causes celebres." Some elements of this *News* story are clearly incorrect. The man who confronted Harvey on the porch with a pistol was the same man who shot Isaiah shortly thereafter, whereas the defense theory in this newspaper article has two men involved in this sequence. It should be noted that official documents related to the England murders contain no reference to Pierce and his brother, to Reverend England killing Pierce, or to Ben Hall and his romantic interest in Susie Taylor. The *Galveston Daily News* article is the only source for this alternate scenario.

29. William Preston Krebs, phone interview, February 24, 2017.

BIBLIOGRAPHY

Abbreviations

GLO   Texas General Land Office Archives

KPCF   Krebs and Preston Executive Clemency File, Texas Secretary of State, TSLAC

NA   National Archives and Records Administration

TSLAC   Texas State Library and Archives Commission

WBTPF   William Barnett Taylor Pension File, National Personnel Records Center, National Archives and Records Administration

Documentary Sources

Ancestry.com

    Arkansas County Marriage Index, 1837–1957

    Carter County, Oklahoma Marriage Records, 1890–1995

    Illinois Marriages, 1790–1860

    Missouri Compiled Marriage Index, 1766–1983

    Missouri, Compiled Marriages, 1754–1850

    Texas Death Certificates, 1903–1982

    Texas Marriage Collection, 1851–1900

    Texas Marriage Index, 1824–2014

Cooke County District Court Records (Gainesville, TX)

David Rumsey Historical Map Collection, https://www.davidrumsey.com

Governor Oran Milo Roberts Papers, Dolph Briscoe Center for American History (Austin, TX)

Joyce E. Whatley Family Genealogy Research Book

Montague County Archives (Montague, TX)

  Montague County Commissioners Court Minutes

  Montague County Court Probate Minutes

  Montague County Court Records

  Montague County Criminal Court Minutes

  Montague County Deed Records

  Montague County District Court Records

  Montague County Police Court Minutes

National Archives and Records Administration (Washington, DC, College Park, MD, and St. Louis, MO)

  1850, 1860, 1870, 1880, 1900, 1910, 1920, 1930 Federal Censuses, Records of the Bureau of the Census, Record Group 29

  Indian Depredation Claims, Records of the United States Court of Claims, Record Group 123

  Maps, Records of the Office of the Chief of Engineers, Record Group 77

  Records of the Adjutant General's Office, 1780–1917, Record Group 94

  Records of United States Army Continental Commands, 1821–1920, Record Group 393

    Letters and Telegrams Sent

    Records of Fort Richardson, TX

    Records of the District of Texas and the Fifth Military District

  Veterans Administration Pension Files

Roscoe P. Conkling Papers, 1904–71, Seaver Center for Western History Research, Natural History Museum (Los Angeles, CA)

Special Collections Library, Sam Houston State University (Huntsville, TX)

Texas General Land Office Archives (Austin, TX)

  Montague County Abstracts

  Montague County Map Drawer

  Young County Map Drawer

Texas Prison Museum (Huntsville, TX)

Texas State Library and Archives Commission (Austin, TX)

  1867–1869 Texas Voter Registration Lists

  Convict Record and Ledger Data Form, Texas Department of Criminal Justice

  Convict Register and Certificate of Prison Conduct, Texas Department of Criminal Justice

  Governor Oran Milo Roberts Papers

  Grayson County Tax Rolls

  Jack County Tax Rolls

  Montague County Tax Rolls

  Pardon Registers, Executive Record Books, 1835–1917

  Texas Ranger and Texas State Troops Muster Roll Index Cards, 1838–1900

  Texas Court of Appeals Minutes

Texas Secretary of State Executive Clemency Records
Wise County Tax Rolls
Young County Tax Rolls
Texas State Preservation Board (Austin, TX)

Interviews

Ariens, Michael. San Antonio, TX, August 20, 2015
Krebs, William Preston. Phone interview, Claremore, OK, February 24, 2017
———. In-person interview, Claremore, OK, December 27, 2018

Newspapers

Austin American-Statesman
Austin Daily Dispatch
Austin Statesman
Austin Weekly Democratic Statesman
Austin Weekly Statesman
Brenham Daily Banner
Daily Ardmorite
Dallas Daily Herald
Dallas Herald
Dallas Morning News
Denison Daily News
Fort Bend Star
Fort Griffin Echo
Fort Worth Democrat
Gainesville Daily Hesperian
Gainesville Hesperian
Galveston Daily News
Graham Leader
San Antonio Daily Express
San Antonio Express
Waco News

Online Sources

Legislative Reference Library of Texas. 2018. https://lrl.texas.gov.
Maurer School of Law, Indiana University. *The Digital Repository.* 2018. https://www
.repository.law.indiana.edu/
Tarlton Law Library, University of Texas, Austin. *Texas Law.* 2018. https://tarlton.law
.utexas.edu
Texas State Historical Association. *Handbook of Texas Online.* 2018. https://www.tshaonline
.org/home/

Published Works

Ariens, Michael. *Lone Star Law: A Legal History of Texas*. Lubbock: Texas Tech University Press, 2011.

Barrett, Thomas. *The Great Hanging at Gainesville, Cooke County, Texas, October A.D. 1862*. Austin: Texas State Historical Association, 1961.

Bates, Edward Franklin. *History and Reminiscences of Denton County*. Denton, TX: McNitzky Printing, 1918. Reprint Denton, TX: Terrill Wheeler Printing, 1976.

Biographical Souvenir of the State of Texas. Chicago: F. A. Battey & Co., 1889.

Blue, Ethan. "A Parody of the Law: Organized Labor, the Convict Lease, and Immigration in the Making of the Texas State Capitol." *Journal of Social History* 43, no. 4 (Summer 2010).

Brown, Gary. *Texas Gulag: The Chain Gang Years, 1875–1925*. Plano: Republic of Texas Books, 2002.

Brown, Richard Maxwell. *Strain of Violence: Historical Studies of American Violence and Vigilantism*. New York: Oxford University Press, 1975.

Carrigan, William D. *The Making of a Lynching Culture: Violence and Vigilantism in Central Texas, 1836–1916*. Urbana: University of Illinois Press, 2004.

Cashion, Ty. *A Texas Frontier: The Clear Fork Country and Fort Griffin, 1849–1887*. Norman: University of Oklahoma Press, 1996.

Cates, Cliff D. *Pioneer History of Wise County*. St. Louis, MO: Nixon-Jones Printing Co., 1907.

Crouch, Barry A., and Donaly E. Brice. *The Governor's Hounds: The Texas State Police, 1870–1873*. Austin: University of Texas Press, 2011.

Crouch, Carrie J. *A History of Young County*. 2nd ed. Austin: Texas State Historical Association, 1956.

DeArment, Robert K. *Bravo of the Brazos: John Larn of Fort Griffin, Texas*. Norman: University of Oklahoma Press, 2002.

Ely, Glen Sample. "Gone from Texas and Trading with the Enemy: New Perspectives on Civil War West Texas." In *Lone Star Blue and Gray: Essays on Texas and the Civil War*, edited by Ralph A. Wooster and Robert Wooster, 160–84. 2nd. ed. Denton: Texas State Historical Association, 2015.

———. *The Texas Frontier and the Butterfield Overland Mail in Texas, 1858–1861*. Norman: University of Oklahoma Press, 2016.

———. *Where the West Begins: Debating Texas Identity*. Lubbock: Texas Tech University Press, 2011.

Gard, Wayne. *Frontier Justice*. Norman: University of Oklahoma Press, 1949.

George, Andrew L. *The Texas Convict: Sketches of the Penitentiary, Convict Farms, and Railroads*. Marion, IL: Leader Print, 1895.

Gillett, James B. *Fugitives from Justice: The Notebook of Texas Ranger Sergeant James B. Gillett*. Austin, TX: State House Press, 1997.

Hamilton, Allen Lee. *Sentinel of the Southern Plains: Fort Richardson and the Northwest Texas Frontier, 1866–1878*. Fort Worth: Texas Christian University Press, 1988.

Hart, Edward Anson. *Twenty-One Years in the Texas Penitentiary, or the Prison Life of Edward Anson Hart*. Stephenville, TX: Frank Leonard, 1900.

Jackson, A. M., and A. M. Jackson Jr. *Cases Argued and Adjudged in the Court of Appeals of the State of Texas*, vols. 3–4. St. Louis: Gilbert Book Co., 1878–79.

———. *Cases Argued and Adjudged in the Court of Appeals of the State of Texas*, vol. 8. St. Louis: Gilbert Book Co., 1880.

Journal of the House of Representatives of the State of Texas. 15th Legislature, 1st Sess. Galveston, TX: Shaw and Blaylock, 1876.

Klugman, Robert H. "Some Factors Affecting the Admissibility of Dying Declarations." *Journal of Criminal Law and Criminology* 39, no. 5 (1949). https://scholarlycommons .law.northwestern.edu/jclc.

Knight, Sherri. *Tom P's Fiddle: A True Texas Tale*. Minneapolis, MN: Langdon Street Press, 2008.

Lau, Timothy T. "Reliability of Dying Declaration Hearsay Evidence." *American Criminal Law Review* 55 (2018): 373.

London, Marvin F. *Famous Court Cases of Montague County*. Saint Jo, TX: SJT Printers, 1992.

———. *Indian Raids in Montague County*. Saint Jo, TX: SJT Printers, 1977.

MacCorkle, Stuart A. "Pardoning Power in Texas." *Southwestern Social Science Quarterly* 15, no. 3 (December 1934): 218–28.

McCaslin, Richard B. *Tainted Breeze: The Great Hanging at Gainesville, Texas, 1862*. Baton Rouge: Louisiana State University Press, 1994.

Memorial and Biographical History of Dallas County. Chicago: Lewis Publishing, 1892.

Neal, Bill. *Getting Away with Murder on the Texas Frontier: Notorious Killings and Celebrated Trials*. Lubbock: Texas Tech University Press, 2006.

Paddock, B. B., ed. *A Twentieth-Century History and Biographical Record of North and West Texas*. 2 vols. Chicago: Lewis Publishing, 1906.

Pagán, Eduardo Obregón. *Valley of the Guns: The Pleasant Valley War and the Trauma of Violence*. Norman: University of Oklahoma Press, 2018.

Paschal, George W. *A Digest of the Laws of Texas*. 2nd ed. Washington, DC: W.H.O.H. Morrison, 1870.

Pearsall, Judy, and Bill Trumble, eds. *Oxford English Reference Dictionary*. New York: Oxford University Press, 2003.

Perkinson, Robert. *Texas Tough: The Rise of America's Prison Empire*. New York: Metropolitan Books, 2010.

Reports of the Superintendent and Financial Agent of the Texas State Penitentiaries Ending October 31, 1888. Austin, TX: Eugene Von Boeckmann, 1889.

Reports of the Superintendent and Financial Agent of the Texas State Penitentiaries Ending October 31, 1890. Austin, TX: Henry Hutchings, 1890.

Reports of the Superintendent and Financial Agent of the Texas State Penitentiaries Ending October 31, 1894. Austin, TX: Ben C. Jones, 1894.

Richter, William L. *The Army in Texas during Reconstruction, 1865–1870*. College Station: Texas A&M University Press, 1987.

Rochette, Patricia Adkins. *Bourland in North Texas and Indian Territory during the Civil War: Fort Cobb, Fort Arbuckle, and the Wichita Mountains*. 2 vols. Broken Arrow, OK: Author, 2005. https://www.bourlandcivilwar.com/.

Rules, Regulations and By-Laws for the Government and Discipline of the Texas State Penitentiaries at Huntsville and Rusk, Texas. Austin, TX: E. W. Swindells, 1882.

Smith, A. Morton. *The First 100 Years in Cooke County.* San Antonio, TX: Naylor Co., 1955.

Steele, Lisa. "Ballistics," in *Science for Lawyers,* edited by Eric York Drogin, 1–30. Chicago: American Bar Association, 2008.

Texas Board of Pardons and Paroles. *Handbook on Parole, Mandatory Supervision, and Executive Clemency.* Austin: Texas Board of Pardons and Paroles, 1978.

Texas State Penitentiaries, Superintendent and Financial Agent Reports for Two Years. Austin: Triplett & Hutchinson, 1888.

Uglow, Loyd M. *Standing in the Gap: Army Outposts, Picket Stations, and the Pacification of the Texas Frontier, 1866–1886.* Fort Worth: Texas Christian University Press, 2001.

Walker, Donald R. *Penology for Profit: A History of the Texas Prison System, 1867–1912.* College Station: Texas A&M University Press, 1988.

Winfrey, Dorman H., and James M. Day, eds. *The Indian Papers of Texas and the Southwest, 1825–1916,* vol. 4. Austin: Texas State Historical Association, 1995.

INDEX

Page numbers in *italics* indicate illustrations.

CPSIA information can be obtained
at www.ICGtesting.com
Printed in the USA
LVHW041831110523
746745LV00004B/624